GW00870345

# Come Listen –

# Sweet Charity Choir

# Come Listen –

# Sweet Charity Choir

## Collated and Edited by
## Kelly Reynolds

Published by Sweet Charity Choir

© Copyright Kelly Reynolds

COME LISTEN – SWEET CHARITY CHOIR

All rights reserved.

The right of Kelly Reynolds to be identified as the author of this work has been asserted in accordance with the Copyright, Designs and Patents Act 1988.

No part of this publication may be reproduced, stored in a retrieval system, or transmitted, in any form or by any means, electronic, mechanical, photocopying, recording or otherwise, nor translated into a machine language, without the written permission of the publisher.

Condition of sale

This book is sold subject to the condition that it shall not, by way of trade or otherwise, be lent, re-sold, hired out or otherwise circulated in any form of binding or cover other than that in which it is published and without a similar condition including this condition being imposed on the subsequent purchaser.

ISBN 978-0-244-79299-2

Book formatted by www.bookformatting.co.uk.

# Contents

# Acknowledgements

Thank you to each and every person who made this book possible - too many to mention.

We are all one big family and together we made this happen.

Thank you

Sweet Charity Choir

All proceeds from this book will go to

Mental Health UK

# Preface

This is a book about what it really means to sing in a choir, a very special choir, which is the brainchild of Jenny Deacon, a uniquely talented and inspirational musician, choir leader and member of the band, The Lounge Kittens.

Sweet Charity Choir under the leadership of Jenny, raises an enormous amount of money for various charitable causes each time they meet, by cake baking, selling and eating, whilst enjoying singing together an amazingly diverse range of songs, stunningly arranged by Jenny herself.

It is widely known that singing in a group makes you feel good but reading the stories within these pages offers a much deeper insight to just how beneficial it really can be as the members relay personal stories, poems, anecdotes and recipes to illustrate the importance of music generally but this choir specifically.

Compiling this book and talking to members has been a humbling and rewarding experience for me. I hope that reading it will make you want to go out and find a choir for yourself, although I defy you to find one as inclusive and giving as Sweet Charity Choir.

Kelly Reynolds

# A Message From
# The Rt Hon Tobias Ellwood MP

As a young boy I knew two things about my uncle: that he was a veteran, and he had taken his own life. Today I'm aware he suffered from depression. Our family knew he was not himself but he found it impossible to battle his demons and, in the end, they defeated him.

I was reminded of him when visiting America last year, for two reasons. The first was the suicides of Kate Spade and Anthony Bourdain, two talented people who seemingly had it all but hid their depression until they could no longer cope. The second was a sight common in the US: complete strangers at an airport approaching a man in uniform and thanking him for his service. I wonder, did anyone ever thank my uncle?

Mental health and well-being is something that I take very seriously, indeed through my Ministerial Role at the Ministry of Defence, I have worked to raise awareness of the dangers of poor mental health. Awareness of ill mental health is essential if we are to combat the detrimental effects that it can have on individuals and their families.

Anyone can suffer from poor mental health, and in many cases the symptoms can be hard to spot. Recent figures published by the Mental Health Foundation for example, indicate that at least two-thirds of us will experience a mental health problem in our lifetimes as a result of stress, anxiety, depression and other factors.

In many cases, people who suffer from poor mental health resist the urge to discuss their feelings or emotions, for fear of ridicule, branding of being 'soft', or not being taken seriously. It is important to note that ignoring mental health issues does not solve the problem, and can in many cases make it worse.

I am sure many, if not all of you, have heard of the old saying 'A problem shared, is a problem halved.' I believe this statement is significantly important when talking about mental health. No one should have to face this alone. It is better to discuss your feelings with someone, whether that be a friend, family member, partner or medical professional, than to leave those feelings unaddressed.

I applaud the courage and bravery of those choir members who have shared their own stories in this book, and I hope they have found it a cathartic experience. I believe having a hobby or interest to focus on which takes you out of yourself for a short time is of vital importance to mental well-being and being part of a group activity is hugely beneficial. Reading some of the stories from members of The Sweet Charity Choir is testament to that.

As patron of several charities including Caring Canines, Dorset ME Support Group and the Samaritans, I congratulate the choir and thank them for the significant amount of money they have raised so far which in turn is helping others and highlighting some of the smaller lesser known charities. I sincerely hope sales of this book do well for Mental Health UK and I wish Sweet Charity every success for the future and hope they continue to raise money for a wide variety of causes.

Finally, there are many avenues and services available for people to utilise if they feel they are struggling from poor mental health. There are some useful addresses at the back of this book plus a list of all the charities to date that the choir has supported. If you are, or know of anyone who is struggling with their mental health, I urge you to speak to someone who can help.

Rt Hon Tobias Ellwood MP

Parliamentary Under Secretary of State and
Minister for Defence People and Veterans

# Foreword
## By Helen Lederer

Many people I know, and I guess many people you know, will have experienced feelings of being in the 'dark' or having the 'black dog'. It is not unusual for many of us to wake up and find an emptiness, lack of purpose or sense of panic. When these feelings present themselves, it is imperative to recognise them, talk about them, learn to manage them and feel that one is not alone.

How brave of people to share their experiences of being in the 'dark' in this amazing collection of writing. Surely, it's through sharing our feelings, that we can feel connected to others – so a big 'hurrah' to all these contributors.

I find a good trick when feeling low is to plan how I am going to spend the next few minutes. Will it be staying still, sorting out a drawer, writing a poem or phoning a friend? I make lists...lots of lists - shopping lists, affirmation lists, to-do lists. And on my to-do lists are usually hugely implausible and unrealistic suggestions of self-improvement. And while taking up hula-hooping and indoor rock climbing never quite materialised during one particularly sad phase, I did find myself booking a singing teacher down the road, just to see if I could make some sounds and change my state of being. Suddenly the scale of C took on a new meaning. And even though I wasn't ON the notes themselves, I had a good go and felt rather transformed afterwards on the way home. By making new sounds, I realised I could challenge my belief system, which is always a good start when dealing with the 'noir'. After a few sessions, I found that doing the (bad) singing was better than being with a therapist! (And believe me, I've dabbled with a wide range of those over the years!)

The act of breathing proves we are alive. Using breath to make a new sound can be powerful stuff....and even more useful is how the ephemerons can start dancing again - particularly after an uninhibited session of Abba songs.

I'm not pitch perfect, but I love pitching imperfectly... and it's free!

Enjoy these courageous, honest and life-affirming pieces....

Helen Lederer

Comedian, Writer and Actress

# A Message Of Thanks
# From Mental Health UK

We would like to say a massive thank you to everyone at Sweet Charity for donating the proceeds of this book to us. The donations you generously give will make a real difference to people's lives.

**What do we do?**

Mental Health UK have supported people affected by mental health problems for over 40 years, including friends, family and carers. We connect with people and organisations to provide advice, information and vital support.

Our support groups can provide a lifeline to someone living with a mental illness who may be feeling isolated. They provide a safe space for people to speak without judgement and try new skills, such as learning guitar. Some of our other wonderful projects include our Mental Health and Money Advice service. The first of its kind, it helps people experiencing both mental health and money problems with clear advice and information. Our 'How does it feel on the inside?' information guides have been sent to over 700,000 GPs and students across the country to date, helping people recognise the signs and symptoms of mental health problems and advise where to seek help.

**1 in 4 people will be affected by a mental health problem every year.**

Everybody has mental health, it's our ever-changing state of well-being. Mental health is just as important as physical health, yet we often don't think about looking after our minds in the same way as our bodies.

Doing things that help us to relax and that we enjoy make a huge difference to our well-being. Whether it's something small like going for a walk or a more creative activity like singing in a choir, looking after our mental health daily can help us to be more resilient and prevent the problems that life throws at us from feeling overwhelming.

Singing in a choir is an incredibly rewarding activity to be a part of. It brings people together to do something fun and creative. It's also a wonderful way to meet new people to support each other and share experiences together.

Sweet Charity's moving 'Come Alive' video on YouTube not only shows their incredible talent but it shines a light on mental health and suicide, an incredibly important topic which is close to many of our hearts.

Thank you again from everyone at Mental Health UK. Your ongoing support and dedication enables us to help more people every day.

Mental Health UK

# Introduction

It's a privilege to be asked to write an introduction for this book. These pages are brimming with positivity and spirit, and flowing throughout is a story of the sometimes profound effects of the Sweet Charity Choir on its members' mental health and well-being.

Mental health is a concept that can be a bit hard to pin down, but we all have it! And we're talking about it more and more: this is such a good thing. My work in public health – which is about the health of populations – means I get involved in all sorts of usually dry and academic analysis which is concerned with people's health and how to improve it. We are recognising that the focus of health and health care has been strongly biased towards treating people's bodies, and we have neglected people's minds and how people feel. But these things can't be divorced from each other. Anyone who has ever had depression can tell you that it affects your body as well as your mind, and we know from scientific studies that having depression doubles the risk of heart disease, for example. Anyone who has a long term condition like diabetes can tell you about the emotional distress that can come with that, and research tells us that those with diabetes are twice as likely to experience depression than those without that condition. These are just a couple of examples which show how mind and body connect in terms of health and illness, and there are many, many more. Some are described in this book.

We are starting to realise that 'mental health' and 'mental illness' are not mutually exclusive. In other words, are those of us who do not have a diagnosable mental illness 'mentally healthy' by definition? Conversely, isn't is possible that even if you have been diagnosed with a psychiatric condition – and hopefully are getting the right treatment and support - you could have mental health, in other words you could have well-being? After all, mental health is defined by the World Health Organisation as:

> "a state of well-being in which every individual realises his or her own potential, can cope with the normal stresses of life, can work productively and fruitfully, and is able to make a contribution to her or his community".

I have known people in my life with a long term mental illness who have had good well-being. They have had appropriate treatment, managed well and enjoyed life, and could be said to be 'flourishing'. Equally, each of us at points in our lives can lack well-being, and at any one time there are many people in our communities who, often because of economic and social burdens, are 'languishing' in a state of emptiness and stagnation (Keyes, 2002, The Mental Health Continuum: From languishing to flourishing, Journal of Health and Social Research). Corey Keyes back in 2002 put forward the idea that regardless of whether or not a person has a diagnosable mental illness such as bipolar, or schizophrenia, or depression, they can be languishing or flourishing.

As a public health specialist interested in mental health, I am very taken with this idea. It identifies a malaise we all see and perhaps experience, which is not mental illness - but neither is it happiness, and it also implies that having a mental illness is not the whole story. It suggests recovery, and the ability to flourish. And it means we should promote positive mental health – for everyone.

Since the work by Keyes, some great research came along called the Five Ways to Well-being (New Economics Foundation (2008) Five ways to well-being https://neweconomics.org/uploads/files/8984c5089d5c2285ee_t4m6bhqq5.pdf). It was produced by the UK's New Economics Foundation and it was based on a detailed analysis of scientific evidence on actions to enhance personal well-being.

Having strong social relationships, being physically active and being involved in learning are all important influencers of well-being, and the processes of giving and becoming more aware have been shown to specifically influence well-being in a positive way. A combination of all of these behaviours will help to enhance individual well-being and may have the potential to reduce the total number of people who develop mental health disorders in the longer term.

*Five Ways to Well-being (graphic from Salford Together,* Five Ways to Well-being http://www.salfordtogether.com/wp-content/uploads/2015/03/Five-ways-to-well-being.jpg)

The well-being-enhancing nature of singing in a group is jumping out from these pages. I have been thinking about the Five Ways as I have read the stories and reflections of the Sweet Charity Choir members. As you read, I challenge you to identify a single one of the Five Ways that is not covered.

Eugenia Cronin MSc, PhD, FFPH
Consultant in Public Health

# Jenny's Story

# Part One

Help for Shirley Portswood

I've got a friend named Shirley Portswood
She should conquer the world, I wish she would
Voice like an angel, extremely musical too
She sticks our choir together, she's our glue
She's a conductor of the highest merit
She's quick and agile like a fluffy red ferret
Everyone loves her, she's got style
She'd do anything for ya, she'll go the extra mile
She's a pretty little thing but she always pulls faces
And she's in a band, it takes her to places
She's got long red hair, when wet it goes curly
And the cutest nose, that's our Shirley
Her musical arrangements are amazing, she's really good
We're all in awe of our Shirley Portswood
She's got us a gig in New York's Carnegie Hall
150 choristers, we're gonna have a ball
Shirley will stand with her hands in the air
Looking like she just don't care
When the music starts she'll come alive
And she'll perform her own version of the hand jive
But it's not just us she has to control
It's not just us giving heart and soul
We have a band, she gives them directions

And an orchestra, brass, woodwind, and string sections
Although she's ready to lead this ensemble
We all need to watch her so our minds won't womble
But there's one thing we need to help our Shirl
She may be a star but she's a normal girl
Talented, inspiring, full of charms
But sadly only has 2 arms!

Jilly Firmin

* * *

I don't remember when I first realised that music was part of my soul. My grandma came to one of my choir sessions recently and was telling everyone that she taught me piano, which isn't true, bless her (she has dementia). She did, however, buy my first toy piano as a birthday present. She couldn't think of what to get me, so Mum suggested a toy piano and, from that, Mum could see that I had really taken to it. When I was four, Mum and Dad bought me my first actual piano, which was fifty quid from a pub down the road. Before I even started lessons, I was listening to theme tunes from cartoons or TV programmes and trying to pick out the notes on the piano. Mum realised I had a naturally musical ear, so I started proper lessons aged four years old.

The piano lessons continued and, when I was about six or seven, we were all offered recorder lessons at school, which I took up and, I have to say, took way more seriously than anyone else! I started with the descant recorder and by the time I was in middle school, I had moved on to the bass. There I was, a tiny little three-foot-nothing girl, playing this huge bass recorder. It must have been quite funny to look at! From then, I began my real musical timeline, starting with the Flute, aged eight, which I took to very quickly and my teacher launched me straight into Grade 3. I continued with that all through middle school and then started learning Saxophone, aged twelve, both Classical and Jazz. I did Grade 5 Jazz Saxophone during my first year at Whitmore High school and by the time I was

2

fourteen, I had achieved Grade 6 Classical, all the while still learning piano and flute and took Grade 8 Flute at the same time with a distinction. At this time, I was a "grunger", so I even taught myself electric guitar. I use that term loosely…

I made it a personal goal that I was going to learn all the instruments in the world to a Grade 1 standard. But life gets in the way, so that hasn't happened…yet! I was quite insular with my voice. I was part of the Harrow Young Musicians, a music service in Harrow which provided me with so much experience and opportunity, and where I learned a lot about discipline, learning and performing as a team and music bringing people together. I joined them when I was eleven in the Intermediate Band, each year moving up into the more senior groups, so by the time I was fourteen I was in Symphonic Winds (the top wind orchestra) as well as the Philharmonic Orchestra (the top full orchestra). I owe a huge amount to HYM; they are currently facing being shut down because of a lack of government funding which makes me incredibly sad. Musical education has played such an important part in my life, without it I wouldn't be where I am today.

When I was thirteen, I embarked on my first musical tour to France with all my friends in the orchestra, which was great! It was also the first time I had ever been away without my parents and the first time I ever got drunk! It was the first time I had experienced a proper social and musical element coming together.

By the time I was 14, alongside school my weekly schedule looked like this:

Wednesday night - HYM Steel Pan Orchestra
Thursday night - HYM Symphonic Wind Orchestra
Friday night - HYM Philharmonic Orchestra

I had formed a lot of close friendships with people who were two or three years older than me at HYM. Whilst I had friends at school, I found it difficult to connect with people in my year, and I was bullied quite a lot. I had an 'older' brain and I think the discipline of music and playing in ensembles with thirty to fifty other people meant that I was far more aware of other people rather than focusing on myself, and at that age at school it's a case of "eat or be eaten" with the ultimate goal of being popular. The teenage years are a very self-absorbed period of time.

Looking back on it now, I can see it was probably down to jealousy. Although I would never have admitted it then, I was talented and that in turn made me different. I wasn't, nor have I ever been, nor will I ever be, an arrogant musician and if ever I even hint at being that way, I would hope my friends and family would tell me to check myself and bring me down to earth. I know my mum would tell me off! I promised myself that I would try to be a humble, giving and kind person and, to people who are insecure, that is a huge threat. All I wanted was to be liked. Even to this day I have always had an inferiority complex, although thankfully not as much now. I have learned to love myself properly over the past two years which is something I have always struggled with.

"Being involved with music was where Jenny was happiest. She could be with like-minded people. Yes, there were a few young divas, but they all worked together as a team and I think that's where Jenny learned the importance of teamwork and she experienced some fantastic achievements at a really early age. As she progressed through the different orchestras, they each had their own tour and when she was fifteen, she went to Italy and played in Venice. Mark Gooding, the Director of Harrow Young Musicians, rushed over to me at the end when we parents were picking them all up and said to me:

"Do you know what your daughter has done?" Of course I didn't, and was expecting to hear dreadful, dreadful things! He went on to tell me:

"She stood up in front of an audience of two thousand people and played an improvised jazz piece on her flute. It was great and she absolutely loved it!"

I was so delighted, and I think that was the moment we realised just how much talent our daughter had, and Mark in

turn realised he had a bit of a protégé on his hands. He began encouraging Jenny to do more solo performances, which for someone whose self-esteem had been hit quite badly, to actually go up there and put yourself in the position of being the focal point was really difficult for her and took a lot of courage. When she was about fifteen or sixteen, Antony (Jenny's brother) and I and some other family members went along to one of the concerts at the Barbican and Jenny was up there playing the flute when suddenly she began singing. I think it was 'Killer Joe'. I mean we had no idea that Jenny could sing and I remember Antony was holding his girlfriend's hand at the time and gradually squeezing it tighter and tighter until she had to ask him to stop!! It really was an "OH MY GOD" moment, and Jenny has never looked back. That is when she really shone. The discipline they all learned at that time was incredible and is the reason Jenny is such a disciplined musician today".
Marion Deacon


I have an ongoing internal battle. On one side is this thing – music - which you know is going to make you feel better, improve your quality of life and make you happy. On the other is the belief that you do not deserve it. Music is the good guy lifting you up, battling the enemy - your low self-esteem - that manifests itself as depression and fights back, all the while telling you that you don't deserve it and you will only feel better for a little while, then you'll feel shit again. Unfortunately, the mental scarring I suffered as a result of the bullying kind of impacted my judgement of people as I got older. I never knew who to trust and I think like many people who have experienced abuse, I became weirdly obsessed with this person who bullied me. It got to the point where I had to have their seal of approval in everything I did. It was such a weird relationship, where they would beat me down, get everyone to give me a really hard time and turn people against me. One minute they would be absolutely vile to me, the next minute this person would click their fingers and everyone would be normal and everything would be fine. I would cling to that feeling of everything being ok and then the fingers would click, and it would start all over again. It was a total power game and they knew it. It was only when I stood up to the ringleader that it stopped. It's like when you go to patient zero of the zombies - if you kill patient zero, the zombies die. I "defeated" the person who was leading it and it really felt like a victory at the time. Once I had stood up to this person, everyone else backed off and my last two years of high school were much better.

> "We were well aware as a family that Jenny was being bullied, and I can remember Antony and I would try to give Jen pep talks to build up her self-esteem, which was really being knocked. We could see she was being intimidated by her peer group. It wasn't fair and it certainly wasn't nice to witness. Antony was bullied too but he dealt with it with humour and he was able to get by. Both Antony and Jenny kept a lot of what was really happening away from us and didn't talk about it. There was one particular time when Antony and I were in the background and encouraged Jenny to stand up for herself with one of the main bullies, which she eventually did and once this person realised they couldn't get to her, they backed off and from then on the bullying all but stopped. It's left its scars though."
> Marion.

For a long time, I have put effort into the wrong people and that has spilled over into my romantic relationships. For whatever reason, be it circumstantial or perhaps because they were just horrible people and I thought that is what I deserved, I have had some really difficult relationships in the past, which I do not want to dwell on, as I am so happy now with my wonderful George.

I tried explaining depression the other day. Sometimes people don't quite understand it and it's not because they don't care, they just do not understand *how* to understand. A physical illness which can potentially take your life away is given more attention because you can SEE it, but you can look at bipolar or schizophrenia in precisely the same way. There are some really major mental illnesses which have a huge impact on your survival, but they sometimes aren't taken seriously because they are "invisible". Some illnesses that aren't life-threatening but life changing like IBS can be (sometimes literally) related to being depressed. Some days you can be absolutely fine, even for weeks and months at a time, then there are times when it knocks you out and you can't move, you can't eat. It lives with you forever and that is what depression is like. It's also a common misconception that if you are depressed you are just a bit 'sad' (a vague expression that frustrates me) - sometimes it's not a case of feeling sad, it's a case of feeling nothing. I experience this a lot.

At twenty-one I went to the doctor, who officially diagnosed me with depression and offered me medication, which I refused. I didn't want it to impact on me as a person. The way I saw it, I had managed to get by in life whilst at the time, not feeling myself. I was able to get out and perform whilst leaving that dark part of myself at home, all the time pretending I was a happy and confident person with no worries, fooling the people who were watching, as well as the people who were teaching me or eventually - when I left University - those who were paying for a service when I was actually earning money from music.

I couldn't let people who had paid for my performance to have it diluted or altered in any way. I have friends who have used anti-depressants and it sometimes zombified them. They seemed to have no control over how the medication affected them, it could leave them glassy-eyed and peacefully existing wherever they were, which I imagine felt relieving, but I just couldn't do that. If I simply existed in my work, people wouldn't learn anything, and they certainly wouldn't have a good time. 99% of the time I could leave my problems at home, go to work, put on my positivity mask and if I needed to cry when I got home then okay, I could cry when I got home.

As for the remaining 1%, these are the rare times when I literally cannot do my job despite my steady progress. I have come on in leaps and bounds since I was first diagnosed, but something happened to knock me back as recently as two weeks ago, which came as a total surprise to me. I feel I have a much better grasp on my patterns and what I need to do to get myself out of a bad place but I had a bad 'trigger' day after meeting with some people I hadn't seen in a while, and one person in particular was not dissimilar to the person in school who caused my first serious problem; it took me right back to being that girl who was bullied at school. I drove home after the event in question feeling utterly worthless but thought to myself: "It's okay, I will just go to bed and I will feel better in the morning". Unfortunately, I woke up and felt worse. I was due to go and teach in London that day and I dreaded going in. George (my partner) was away at a gig, so I was just wandering around the house alone randomly bursting into tears, all the while conscious that I had to go and do my job. I eventually got in my car to leave and got half-way there and started falling apart. I arrived there and just sat in my car for half an hour, crying, but eventually went upstairs to teach them. As I went in and looked at everyone waiting for me it was the first time in my life, let alone my career, where I thought: "I just cannot do this." The thought of standing there in front of them and having to teach them made me feel sick. I started sweating and burst into tears and ran out of the room. Luckily, I was surrounded by a wonderful group of NHS workers and supporters, and it was the best environment I could have been in to go through that.

Anyone who has been affected by traumatic events, in any circumstances, will understand that sometimes something happens which triggers that traumatic memory and throws you back into the place that you were at the time that it happened. You immediately question your actions, if you've acted wrongly, if you're about to get hurt, and kind of takes you out of reality. And it's a constant cycle. When things are going particularly well, I am always waiting for something to go wrong, and for history to repeat itself - it's just the nature of the beast. It's important to recognise that you are going to experience those kinds of ups and downs if you are diagnosed with an illness, whatever it is.

8

Over the years, I have come to realise that there's almost always something going on behind closed doors and as such I have come to appreciate that this can affect people's behaviour. There will always be difficult people in life, but if you can think about them as a person on their own with a separate life to that moment in time, it's far easier to understand that they are often just lashing out about something else. I didn't speak publicly about my depression until I was a few years into my Rock Choir journey, (about 25 years old) but I found it therapeutic to express myself, and having the knowledge that people knew about it and knew where they stood with me made me feel I could be more myself. I sometimes wonder how many people I interact with on a weekly basis are harbouring their troubles, I absolutely hope that being in the choir environment has given people courage to speak out (I think this book speaks for itself!)

Choir leading was never on my radar and I never sang in a choir when I was younger. My first solo performance was when I was fifteen at the Barbican, so I didn't really start singing properly until I was sixteen, and even then, I didn't take my voice seriously. It wasn't until I was nineteen in my first year at Southampton University that I took to the stage in my first ever Musical Theatre performance, playing Lucy in *You're A Good Man Charlie Brown*. The character of Lucy was tone deaf, so I had to pretend for the whole show that I couldn't sing (which is actually incredibly hard to do!) After this I musically directed a few more shows and auditioned to be the Assistant Conductor of the Concert Band, having never conducted before. I wanted to learn and found it so enjoyable that I began to realise that I could teach. By my third year I was in two Orchestras and was the Musical Director (MD) of the Southampton University Jazz Orchestra (SUJO). I still hadn't conducted a choir though.

"I remember she danced when she conducted the orchestra at the Turner Sims Concert Hall and my dad cried when he saw her. The orchestra received a standing ovation, but it was as much for Jenny as for anyone else. There were a lot of

bigwigs at that concert. The Director of the National Theatre came over afterwards, having seen my dad crying. He was so impressed and told me they had never before seen a standing ovation for the orchestra. It was absolutely wonderful".
Marion


Being the MD and conducting the SUJO allowed me to feel like I was completely connected to the music, because I channelled the pulse and energy of the music through my body, into my conducting, which then transferred to the musicians. It was like magic. That night conducting at the Turner Sims Concert Hall was one of the best nights of my whole life. I loved every second and felt validated. At the time SUJO didn't have the best reputation and I really whipped everyone into shape.

I originally wanted to be an Orchestra Flautist and spent years focussing on that being my future, until my third year of University when I asked my tutor what the next stage was of getting into music college.

"Oh, you won't get in," she replied.

"Oh! Umm why?" was all I could say. I was completely taken aback.

"You won't get in because you do too much. You have spread your ability across so many different avenues that you don't meet the standard as the other flautists, you're just not good enough. It is a cut-throat industry and difficult to get into and, if you had poured all of your efforts solely into the flute, it would have been fine, but knowing who you are, I don't think you would be happy doing that."

I was so angry with her at the time. I thought she had destroyed my dream and all the hard work I had put in over 15 years. But, of course, she was totally right.


"Jenny's response to that was: 'Up yours! I'm going to prove you wrong!' and she promptly got a First in her recital that night"
Marion

(I fully appreciate everything my University flute teacher had taught me, and the 'up yours' is that of a petulant student). I think a lot of that 'First' came from the staff who saw how much work I had put in. I have listened back to the recording of my recital since and I genuinely don't think I deserved that mark, but I think they respected me as a musician.

I started a Masters in Composition, but didn't feel very connected to it. I think the idea of having a solitary job put me off and composition didn't appeal to me as much as directing did after my varied previous year. During this year, I started looking for jobs so I could make some money. I got my first MD job for a one-off Christmas performance, and then became the MD of the Mountbatten Players for 2 years. Here I had to teach the cast the music but also had to write and arrange the whole score for a ten-piece band, which I discovered I could easily do. So, I could write arrangements and enjoyed directing people. What next? My boyfriend at the time found an audition advertised for Rock Choir and encouraged me to go for it. I still have the email from him asking if I might be interested in the job!

# Jenny's Quirky Questions

*Q - If you could teleport, what year/era would you go to?*

A - Hmm… Question - would I be **living** in this era? My problem is, there are so many interesting portals of time if you are a man! Most periods in history pre 1960 were RUBBISH if you were a woman with very little freedom and creativity.

That's a boring feminist start to an answer, isn't it? Okay. I would love to portal back to the middle of the Golden Age of Hollywood. It would have been so exciting to witness the amount of movies produced in this time with all the glitz and the glam, more specifically the 1940s because there would be the addition of Swing music - I would have loved to have met Count Basie.

*Q - What person from history would you like to be?*

A - I strongly relate to Ludwig van Beethoven - he is my musical idol. His disregard for the 'rules' not only of compositional creativity but how he achieved it, totally speak to my soul and my approach to music.

When he eventually became deaf, he used his inner musical knowledge and instinct to create some of the best and most acclaimed music he wrote in his history. To be able to understand something with such a literal barrier is something I also relate to - I don't have the most extensive musical knowledge but I truly understand the way something should sound and how to achieve it. Also, he had a good soul and composed for who and what felt right. His final 9th Symphony ("Ode to Joy") was 'an optimistic hymn championing the brotherhood of humanity' which is basically what I base my whole career/ethos on.

*Q - Marmite - love it or hate it?*

A - EMPHATICALLY LOVE IT.

I used to be a very fussy eater and Marmite and Cheese sandwiches were the only sandwiches I would eat for about 8 years. It is still my favourite sandwich to date. (I implore Marmite lovers to try Marmite, cheese and cheese and onion crisp sandwiches. DO IT.)

*Q - If a film was made of yourself, who would you choose to play you ?*

A - Tina Fey. I have been compared to her so many times in the past 10 years of my life that there simply isn't another person that could play me.

Not only is she (apparently) my Doppleganger, I totally respect her as a comedian, actor, writer and general good person.

*Q - Most embarrassing moment ?*

A - My oldest and newest most embarrassing moment are both wee related.

Oldest - I was 10 years old (that's embarrassing on it's own..) I first discovered Karaoke on holiday in Majorca. After watching my dad expertly sing "Whisky In the Jar" I decided to have a go. I found ALL THE SONGS FROM GREASE (I was obsessed with it that year, watching it every day in the Summer Holidays) and chose "Hopelessly Devoted to You", singing along with the words I was transported into the film itself, singing my little heart out. What I failed to realised was everyone staying at the hotel complex were watching and exploded into applause when I finished, causing me to spin round in shock and wet myself in front of them all. Cue the tears. Cue mum having to rush over and rescue me from deer-inheadlights shock standing in my own urine. The worst part was having to face the hotel guests afterwards… HOWEVER I now use this story as an icebreaker to anyone who is trying out the choir for the first time and might be a bit nervous. "Have you wet yourself? NO? Well you're doing better than I did!"

Newest - Having a really big corporate singing teaching job for Youtube alongside a terrible bladder infection when cystitis struck and I ended up having to…. Hold myself… in front of my big events company boss when trying to find a toilet in the car park before said big corporate job… It was the first time I'd ever met him as well. Luckily, they still employ me for events! HUZZAH!

Kids, IT'S IMPORTANT TO STAY HYDRATED.

*Q - Where do you see yourself in 10 years?*

A - I see myself still teaching my lovely Sweet Charity choirs but also travelling the world and teaching communities to sing and support together.

I would love to learn about the musical cultures and traditions across the globe and find a way to combine my love for music and people by giving people the tools to support themselves when in need and to use their skills to benefit others. George and I will still have our cat family.

*Q - Whats your favourite musical ?*

A - I am always going to have a soft spot for *Company* by Steven Sondheim - I learned so much about myself and my ability as a performer, the music is so beautiful, the actors I worked alongside were superb, I met Timia on this musical which put me on a path I was never expecting(!) And I won an award for 'Best Supporting Actress'. I ESPECIALLY loved the latest recreation in the West End where many of the gender roles were reversed and altered, in particular having the lead 'Bobby' as a woman TOTALLY refreshed some very outdated ideas of relationships and marriage.

I also love *The Last 5 Years* by Jason Robert Brown, the storyline is so brutal and the music is the kind of music I wish I could even think of, let alone write! It's proper 'jazz face' music!

*Q - If you could collaborate with any musician, alive or dead, who would it be?*

A - Too many to list!

  Acoustic, bare beauty - Eva Cassidy. My vocal idol. Her musicality, timing, tone, timbre, harmonic use, I would have loved to have seen her live. She's the queen of vocals to me.

  Rock - Dave Grohl, he's such an involved musician AND a perfectionist, I would love to sit down and work something out with him, although I think we would be in the studio for DAYS making it just right.

  Pop - Clean Bandit. I'm such a fan of their music, they write the catchiest songs and I love their use of counter melodies and electronic polyphony. It's really detailed!

  Jazz - Frank Sinatra or Tony Bennett. Their voices are so different and yet both achieve the buttermelting feeling when I hear them sing. I would love to riff and ad lib. with them both.

For song-writing I would love to sit in a room with Frank Turner and watch him work, he tells stories that I listen to (and if you know me, you'll know I rarely listen to lyrics, they're just bypassed when it comes to the melody and harmony when I hear) and seamlessly connects them to his music. Some songs break my heart, others make me feel I could do anything.

*Q - Favourite Cocktail ?*

A - I love a Moscow Mule. Vodka, ginger beer and lime. PERFECTION.

*Q - Outside of music what do you do to relax?*

A - I recently started vlogging! (Video-blogging) I started because I wanted to do something that a) stopped me working around the clock

Helped me to exercise vocalising my thoughts and opinions

Improved my quality of life by doing more, seeing more and FEELING more

Vlogs range from musical adventures, tours, bucket list adventures, family shenanigans, general musings, films reviews and day to day blatherings. The ultimate goal is to have enough skills and know-how to create memory book blogs for when George and I commit to long travelling periods throughout the years to come.

My Youtube Channel is Jen Kitten Thoughts in case anyone was interested in watching them.

*Q - What would you tell your 13 year old self ?*

A - This could go very deep…

I would tell 13 year old me to love herself. To be herself with her head held high instead of hanging it in doubt, because the people who question her are the people who wish they were like her. I've been bullied all my life in some shape or form and whilst it still hurts, I wish I could have primed myself better when I was younger.

*Q - What song do you wish you'd written?*

A - Probably Bohemian Rhapsody by Queen, or Rhapsody in Blue by Gershwin. Both of them are epic pieces of art. I love a Rhapsody!

*Q - What is the funniest thing that has happened to you on stage?*

A - I burped and consequently dribbled on myself in front of 250 people once. I laughed at myself for a good few minutes without anyone but the few people who saw it in the front row knowing what the ruddy hell was going on!

*Q - If there was one new invention that would make your life easier or fun, what would it be?*

A - Probably having a car that ran on farts. With help from George we'd travel the world for free!

*Q - Desert Island Discs - which 8 discs, book and luxury item would you choose ?*

A - Discs

Linkin Park 'Hybrid Theory'
Gordon Goodwin's Phat Band 'Swingin' for the Fences'
Best of Abba
Now that's what I call music 37
Frances 'Things I never said'
Incubus 'Make Yourself'
Bad News 'Bad News'
Sibelius and Beethoven Symphonies

Book - The Jazz Theory Book by Mark Levine, so I can keep my mind busy and active!
Luxury Item - A BLANKET. I ALWAYS NEED A BLANKET

*Q - Without spilling the beans, what is your 5 year plan?*

A - Hmm... okay, not spilling the beans....
Perform overseas again

Perform in a few big spaces with lots of people in the UK
Make some new friends
Record some music
Um. Yeah. That will do…

*Q - Who would you like to swap places with for 24 hours?*

A - I'm very inspired by a friend I had at University called Holly Madge. She has a unique and perfect blend of being beautiful inside and out, she's an insanely talented drummer and percussionist, she started her own business and plays for some of the biggest musicians, composers, artists and events around the world. She's incredibly grounded, fiercely independent and driven, so easy to get on with, always striving to learn and do more and follows her heart. If I could spend 24 hours in her mind, I would learn some of the strength and courage that she has had from the past 10 years to move forward in the next 10 of my own.

*Q - What's your favourite food/meal ?*

A - Toad in the Hole. I love Yorkshire puddings. I would eat them every day if I could. Also, the sausages HAVE to be Richmond Sausages. I know, I know. Sausage specialists would say I'm mad for saying this, because they're 'not real sausages' but I think they're the tastiest.

*Q - If you could meet one musician/icon dead or alive for a chat, who would you choose?*

A - Gordon Goodwin - I absolutely love the music he composes for the Gordon Goodwin Phat Band, I would love to pick his brains on how he writes and how he came to know all the amazing musicians in his band!

*Q - Who would you like to perform a duet with?*

A - Male vocal - Stevie Wonder or Chris Cornell - 'nuff said.

Female vocal - Frances. She gives me total chills, and her harmony writing is exceptional.

*Q - What's the most important decision you've ever made ?*

A - I think deciding to go to University to study music. I took a gap year and was originally going to study Music Technology in Lancaster, when someone said to me in passing conversation "Why are you doing that when you're a musician?" And they were totally right. My musical spark had disappeared for a few years when I turned 17/18 and it wasn't until I started talking to people about music degrees and Universities that it came back. I was VERY late to be applying to new Universities (in June to start in September) and my friend Rupal told me how wonderful Southampton University was. I went to visit and fell in love with it. The moment I drove by the campus I knew it was the place for me and when I walked around the music department I could see my future beginning down its hallways. I was extremely lucky to get a place there as I didn't technically have the correct grades to get in (as I say... I lost my spark aged 17/18) but they must have seen some sort of potential in me... and for that I'm eternally grateful. I wouldn't be where I am without being at Southampton University for a plethora of reasons.

*Q - If you didn't get into music, what would you have done ?*

A - When I was a child I wanted to be a vet! And then the sudden realisation that I wouldn't be able to save them all made me cry so I decided to give that idea up...

I think if I didn't get into music I would have gotten into acting. I'm still *slightly* sad that it didn't end up being a part of my life, but you never know! I've still got years left in me with a rubber face, think of all the weirdo crazy lady parts I could play on screen!

*Q - What is your greatest fear ?*

A - Wasps. I hate the things. Even the sound of wasps makes me feel physically sick. I'm mildly allergic to them so the stings hurt that much more but they're horrible, horrible creatures that only minimally pollinate flowers... Urgh. That fact alone means they have to stay but I'm SO frightened of them. I've only ever been brave in the face of a wasp once in my life; when I was working in a performing arts camp in America, one of the girls in my 'dorm' was DEATHLY allergic to wasps and was being 'chased' by one, so I threw myself in front of her until the wasp started chasing me. Then I ran away screaming like a little girl.

*Q - What's your favourite cake?*

A - Carrot Cake. It's the best. Get in my face.

*Q - How many instruments do you play ?*

A - Oooh good question!
Piano
Flute
Piccolo
Clarinet (Just about)
Oboe (Grade 1 baby!)
Soprano, Alto, Baritone Saxophone (I could never master the Tenor Sax)
Guitar (Basic)
Trombone (also Grade 1 baby!)
Steel Pans
Basic training in percussion.
So if you count all the saxophones and group percussion as one instrument. 12! I wish I knew more. I have a viola that was given to me as a graduation present... only been touched once.
CHALLENGE ACCEPTED!

*Q - Borneo, Japan or Bali ?*

A - Japan. Hands down. Every time. I am so incredibly desperate to go to Japan. There is so much history, interesting culture and traditions, urban and rural landscapes and ways of life, plus the weird and the wonderful. It's top of my list to go!

*Q - How long to do an arrangement?*

A - It really depends on the type of song and whether it requires an extensive harmony arrangement to honour the original or whether it is a fun and upbeat perfect pop song that writes itself! Sometimes I can write full song choral arrangements in about 3 hours, others a couple of days and sometimes they can take weeks.

You'll be surprised to know that sometimes it doesn't actually make a difference if I know the song well or not, some songs just 'translate' better than others.

*Q - How many cats do you think you will own in your lifetime ?*

A - Oh my goodness who knows!? We have 2 right now. And they'll be here FOREVER (waaa)

I reckon there will be at least another 4 at least. I want to rescue them all.

# A Standing Ovation For
# Our Professional Musical Musings

Take a Leap

I joined a choir many years ago
I wasn't sure but thought I'd dip my toe
Such good fun so I dived right in
And now I go weekly to make a din
I'm proud to say not one I've missed
The benefits are amazing, a great long list
My health wasn't good but choir repaired it
I made many friends and our singing, we shared it
My mental health was good but now it's great
I've done so much stuff I think it was fate
Any loneliness soon dissipates
With all my friendly choir mates
Little did I know where that first step would lead
For me it's not a want, it's a need
I don't know what I'd do without singing
All the friendships and performances it's bringing
And top of the pile of joy is our lovely Jen
She brings such love to all the ladies and men
Quirky, cheeky, second to none
I've never known someone impart so much fun
And charity fund raising for serious issues
Her arrangements are sick, we often need tissues

They touch the soul and the heart so deep
Everyone should do it, take a leap!

Jilly Firmin

**Jaret Reddick**
**Bowling For Soup**

To be known as the funny guy your entire life puts an awkward spin on finding out you have depression. I was always good in crowds. Those close to me say it is like a switch...I can turn it on in an instant. And I am not being fake. I am just putting forward what people expect to see and hear. Because if I didn't do that, well, something would be wrong, wouldn't it? I would be "an asshole." Or worse, "boring!"

Admitting I am a human being is something I had to do first. But it took four years. Four years of the anxiety I had felt for so long taking the wheel. See, I didn't know it was anxiety. I didn't know I was depressed. Especially the anxiousness, it had been there, popping its head out for a long time. But I didn't have a clue about its power. So when it got me, I thought I was being lazy. I thought I needed more motivation. As if a successful career and awesome family weren't enough motivation. So I stopped moving. Stopped working. Stopped smiling. Got fat. Got more depressed.

Became more anxious. And then just kept repeating.

I am a human being. Though in my own head space, I might be a super hero. I might think I am the smartest person in the room. The happiest person on the planet. Well, I am not. And that is fine.

You can't do it alone. Even if you think you are, you aren't.

Talk to your friends. Talk to your doctor. GO TO COUNSELING if you can!!

There is not one solution. No magic pill. But there is relief for you out there. It's there. I promise it is there.

The combination of meds, therapy and communication helped me. But none of it would have done anything if I hadn't admitted I am only human. And we all need a little help every now and then. Some of us just didn't need it until we were forty-two years old.

Take care of you

**George Say**
**Drummer and Jen's Partner**

Being Jenny's partner I feel extremely privileged to be able to see what goes on behind the scenes of Sweet Charity Choir, to be an observer if you will. I see the sweat and tears that go into what Jenny does for Sweet Charity and all of its members and the extremely productive late nights fuelled by all the tea I have to make! I also see the pure joy and happiness she creates in every single person in the choir, and their fierce loyalty to her.

Her message is one of kindness to others, giving to those in need, having a real laugh, generally enjoying life as much as you can whilst sparking joy in those around you. Sweet Charity provides something that nothing else can and it's so addictive!

Before meeting Jenny, I had no idea of her capabilities as a musician, a choir leader or as a therapist, because that's what I believe she is, someone who wants to help and see others as happy as they can be. I've met people who tell me they need their Jenny fix and I can totally see why! The first time I saw her as a leader I was in extreme awe. I couldn't take my eyes off of her and neither could anyone else. She is a truly inspirational woman, musician and leader.

And as for the unbelievable choir that she has created, they could easily be professional. Jenny knows how to get the best out of people and her hilarious explanations and anecdotes on how notes should sound absolutely have a method behind their madness! There really is only one Jenny Deacon!

On the side of the observer I have been there talking to members that have been having a rough day, a rough week or a really worrying life situation that they can't stop thinking about right up until the point they open their mouths to sing and I observe them transform into something else. I see Jenny do or say something funny and I see the genuine laughter, joy and smiles on people's faces. They let go of everything in the world that bothers them and be completely in the now of the moment and the music and just sing, and it's so beautiful to observe.

I've seen people travel for over 3 hours to be in one of Jenny's choir sessions, sometimes on a weekly basis, I've seen people show up on their own, terrified of what to expect and end up feeling so comfortable with everybody in the room and enjoying it so much that they have joined in their first session! I've experienced first-hand the effects Sweet Charity Choir and Jenny has on people and it's absolutely magical. I can only speak on behalf of myself, but the Sweet Charity Choir members and Jenny have certainly made me a better person and changed my life for the better and I'm certain it has done the same for others too. I've also been introduced to friends for life.

Sweet Charity Choir isn't just about singing. It's about truly living, giving, family, joy and taking your life into an exciting direction and experiencing amazing things you never thought possible.

**Kerry Ellis**
**West End and Broadway Star**

I have worked with so many choirs over the years and see what a joyous community they create. There is nothing better than seeing a group of friends working as a team on stage with such a love of singing. I have been very fortunate to have had a wonderful career playing incredible roles and have performed all over the world but, in all honesty, it's always been better when I have been able to share the experience with someone. Having fellow cast members to work with, bounce off and support each other is what it's all about, and I can only imagine that's what it's like being part of a choir.

On a personal note, I love singing with a choir. I have had choirs on most of my solo tours and with my dear friend, Dr. Brian May, we also had choirs on our tours. They bring so much to a show; the energy, fun and sound of course is magical, you can't beat it!!!

**Nicky Stevens**
**Brotherhood of Man –**
**Eurovision song contest winners for the UK 1976**

Many years ago I was in an abusive relationship and the victim of mental cruelty. To add to this my lovely dog was killed by a car on Christmas Day. These two experiences caused me to suffer from anxiety and depression which was to last nearly eight years. Anti-depressants did not work for me and alcohol was a no, as the effects would only add to the situation, making it worse. It was a tremendously difficult time for me. I found that it was easier to put on a false smile in front of people. How do you explain an invisible illness?

"I am suffering from anxiety and stress," I told a few.

"What have you got to be depressed about?" was the usual answer. "You have a wonderful talent and a successful career."

No one understood why hiding away in bed covered with a

duvet and the curtains drawn would be my preferred option of how to spend my day.

I believe that singing with Brotherhood of Man greatly helped me through this time. When I was singing, somehow I felt lifted. It is a known fact that your breathing technique as a vocalist takes more oxygen into your body and circulates, helping to release endorphins from the brain producing a feel good factor. It makes you happy even if it is only for a short while and can be a temporary release from that dreadful feeling you have to wake up with every day.

As well as still performing as part of Brotherhood of Man, I am also a singing teacher and choir conductor, so I can fully empathise with what Jenny and the Sweet Charity Choir members are all saying in this book. My own choir members tell me that community singing makes them feel uplifted and happy. Conducting them using my musical knowledge and experience makes me happy too and creates a strong sense of connection. For me there is nothing like the sound of that wall of voices travelling towards you. I have called the choir 'Sing 2B Happy' which is very apt because whenever I am involved in singing of any type, it is a happy me. My advice to people is to try singing. It doesn't matter if you have the worst voice in the world, it might be just what you need in your life. Many people join choirs because they want to sing but are perhaps scared to sing solo, preferring that their voice is hidden. So what? The main thing is YOU will know that you are singing and hopefully by doing so, feeling the benefit and enjoying yourself.

## David Morgan Young
## Theatre Director/Choreographer

David Morgan Young (left) and Michael Rose (right)

Back in the early eighties, I performed in a T.I.E (Theatre in Education – as it was called then) play called SNAP OUT OF IT. A musical piece on mental health, satirising the problems with doctors just giving out pills and not dealing with or helping the real problem of the individual. We toured schools and arts centres.

After one particular performance, a teacher came up to us and thanked us for the show, saying it was the first time she had cried in five years. She hadn't been able to release her feelings and emotions this way. The piece had helped her deal with the problems she had.

I remember, back in the day, when I was depressed and would curl up on the sofa and sleep to try and make it go away. I would be told: 'snap out of it' or 'pull yourself together'.

It took many months of sleepless nights, literally still awake as the dawn came up, and a job to help me through that time. We all need a purpose to get up in the morning. Whether that be work, family, children or pets. It's good to be needed.

Care, time, education and knowledge is needed to help and support.

## The Neuroscience of Singing

In other words, what goes on in our minds, bodies and hearts when we sing - the science behind what we know instinctively.

During the late 1970,s and 1980,s, the development of scanners such as CT and MRI have enabled scientists to look inside our brains and bodies to discover what happens when we think about different things or do different tasks. So I decided to see what happens to each of us when we sing in unison and harmony as part of the Sweet Charity Choir.

I have summarised my findings as people have written whole books on this stuff.

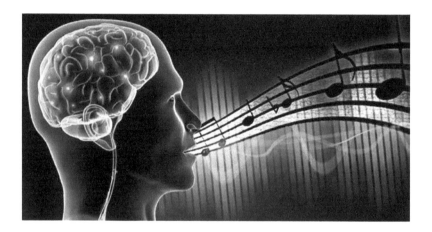

Our brains light up like a Christmas tree

Whether we are actually singing or just thinking about singing, studies have shown that pretty much all parts of our brains are lit up and active. We are activating the Broca's area in the front brain that deals with language. The auditory and muscle memory circuits are abuzz and the hippocampus area is busy recalling and recording and learning. This helps us develop neuroplasticity, which is the ability to organise and make new connections at a physiological level in our brains. In other words the physiology of how we learn.

Our creative juices are quite literally flowing along these neural pathways. Creativity is what enables us to invent new paths for ourselves by solving our problems and creating new plans.

Hormones are flooding our bodies

All sorts of hormones are being released into our bodies on the instructions of a part our brains called the Amygdala. The amygdala is an almond shaped set of neutrons located deep in the centre of our brain. It plays a key part in processing our emotions, memory and levels of arousal and is part of the limbic system.

The hormones /chemicals produced when we sing include

Oxytocin – The love drug. This is produced when we feel loved and bonds us together. It is part of sexual reproduction and is produced before and after childbirth to aid bonding. It helps produce the feeling of love.

Serotonin – This is the well-being or happy drug found mostly in the brain, bowel and platelets. Serotonin is used to transmit between nerve cells and it is thought to be active in smoothing tense muscles. It is also a precursor to melatonin which regulates the body's sleep/wake cycle. Low levels of Serotonin are linked to depression.

Endorphins – The natural pain and stress fighters. They are structurally similar to the drug morphine, and they activate opioid receptors in the brain that help minimise discomfort. They can help bring about feelings of euphoria and general well-being.

Adrenalin – The energy drug. This enlivens our bodies by increasing heart rate and blood pressure, expanding our lungs and dilating our pupils. It often gets a bad press as too much adrenaline can be overwhelming and is a sign of stress. However, the right levels (which we get when we sing) creates a heightened state of physical and mental alertness… or what I call "a buzz".

Dopamine – The feel good hormone and is associated with feelings of euphoria, bliss, motivation and concentration. Dopamine plays a part in controlling our movements and emotional responses. It is vital to physical and mental well-being.

Breath-work

Singing involves steadying and deepening our breath, a kind of breath work out. Universally this is known to relax muscles and calm our minds from the stresses of everyday life. Breathing deeply increases our oxygen intake and brings an aliveness to our physiology. We release tension and gain energy at the same time.

Anatomy

We become much more aware of our physical selves, our focus goes to our bodies when we sing. We develop muscle memory that helps us find the right note (that's why Jenny gets us to repeats short sections … there is a clear purpose behind it!). We learn to breath more efficiently using our diaphragms, to sit up or stand in a way that allows our chests to expand for singing.

Singing bonds us together

If you look at the history of singing in a group it started with tribal singing which was a way of building support, transmitting important information and warding off enemies. Instinctively we have known how important singing is to our sense of community, which is why it is intertwined with our daily lives. You will find it extremely hard to go a whole day without hearing singing … it is everywhere and of course it is often in our heads too.

Research shows that when we sing in a choir not only are we listening, harmonising our voices and movements to produce these beautiful sounds, but our heartbeats physically attune to each other... how cool is that! Our hearts are all beating together.

We are literally attuning and bonding when we sing at Sweet Charity. When we sing, we change our whole selves in mind, body and heart.

In a nutshell, neuroscience provides the evidence behind the claims that singing is beneficial.

Taken from the work and teachings of Tania De Jong AM and Professor Sarah Wilson, Melbourne University.

**Some Of The Benefits Of Singing**

**(I am sure there are loads more that you can think of.....)**

Increases self-confidence and self esteem
Provides an opportunity for personal expression or finding your voice
Decreases stress and comforts us
Develops and enhances memory
Helps us to stave off neurological disorders like dementia
Develops language and other skills like planning and organising
Develops speech and helps heal speech problems
Reduces loneliness
Increases our blood flow
Helps heal strokes
Relieves the symptoms of depression
Augments social bonding and empathy by developing feelings of support and safety
Benefits your heart and increases energy
Fosters clear thinking and correct breathing
Lifts our hearts and spirits

Helps us recover physically and emotionally from trauma and injury

"Overall singing makes us smarter, healthier, happier and more creative and when we sing with other people this effect is amplified."
Mila Redwood
Founder of Sing for Joy.

Kim Hamilton
Counsellor and EMDR Practitioner
Sweet Charity Choir Member

**What singing and music means to me …..**

"Singing is as old as the hills. It is innate, ancient and within all of us. It really is one of the most uplifting therapeutic things we can do."
Katie Kat
US Opera singer

"Music has healing power. It has the ability to take people out of themselves for a few hours."
Elton John

"Music shows us that every story within every voice matters."
Michelle Obama
The Grammys, February 2019

"Songs change a lot. Music lifts the spirits, crosses boundaries and can move people to do things they would not otherwise have done."
Joan Baez
The Observer, 24/2/19

"Music has always been like a healing balm for me. I know that I can always find joy there."
John Grant, Musician
The Observer, 17/2/19

"Singing creates an amazing feeling of unity. It's what everyone in Britain should do right now. Not in their thousands. In their millions."
Mirga Gratzinyte-Tyla,
Conductor of the City of Birmingham Symphony Orchestra.
Quoted from The Observer, 24/03/2019

"The first breath a choir takes together, a breath filled with focus, intention and emotion, a breath unified for no other reason than to make something beautiful together…that is the reason we do what we do."
Eric Whitacre
American Composer,
Conductor and Creator of
the worldwide Virtual Choir

"Music is what feelings sound like."
Georgia Cates
Author

# A Huge Round Of Applause Please
# As The Bass Section Take A Bow

Sungover

A hangover. You've heard of that, everyone knows
But today I haven't got one of those
I really don't know what to do
That's why I'm here asking you
Yesterday I sang some songs
And it went on all day long
We usually meet each month as a group
We're Jenny's singing charity troop
We're called Sweet Charity, that's our name
And we sing our hearts out, that's our game
But it was something special yesterday
We knew it would be good come what may
We recorded songs Jenny's taught us through the year
And many of us shed a tear
That girl is special, her arrangements are sick!
With her teaching skills we sound so slick
Freedom, Faith, Come Alive, to name a few
We nailed it, really, who knew?
Andy and Kurt with their weeping guitars
And George the best drummer ever, by far
The best musicians money can buy
And Olli the magnificent sound guy
There to record us as we sang with feeling

And today my head is still reeling
Taking snaps and recording, Marianne and Scott
While in the kitchen the Mamas were getting hot
Big thanks to Mama Deacs and Mama Say
Their cooking kept us going all day
And Colin was there to do Jenny's bidding
And wasn't he looking good (Colin, you know I'm only kidding)
And not least the choir who made all that noise
All the lovely girls and boys
We all sang out to our hearts content
And every word we all meant
Jenny 'you've been sucha, sucha good friend'
We all know singing can help to mend
Anxiety, stress, depression too
And for us it's all down to you
So today I feel 'Sungover' from an exhilarating day
But I'm sure everyone would love to say
THANK YOU JENNY XXX

Jilly Firmin

**My Singing Journey**

My journey singing with Jenny started in 2014 and I have been with Sweet Charity since our very first Workshop.

Having sung in my school choir, singing was something I wanted to do for "me". A friend suggested I join her at Rock Choir and once I had met Jenny and seen how singing can bring people together and foster new relationships I was hooked. Since my divorce I had lost my confidence and I have a very stressful and demanding job as well as being a mum, so singing is the only time I don't think about work and other problems. I can just immerse myself in the music while having fun with friends.

It turned out to be great timing as six months after I started singing my daughter was diagnosed with an eating disorder and we went through a traumatic couple of years. All my time, energy and emotion were invested in supporting her and being there for her – but I tried desperately to keep singing as I needed to keep myself strong.

Without knowing the details my choir friends have got me through which has also helped my daughter to get through. At the lowest point, at some rehearsals I literally maintained text contact with her the whole way through, but I needed my outlet. We say at Sweet Charity that we sing together supporting others; but by supporting each other we are also helping to support our families and friends as well as our charities.

I wouldn't change a minute of my singing journey. I have never felt so much love in the room as when we come together to sing and I have never met such an accepting, loving group of people as our Sweet Charity family, led by Jenny, who inspires us all to do better, be better and help each other.

Anon

* * *

I find it quite difficult to express what choir means to me and the impact it has had on my life. I have been a member of Rock Choir for a number of years, having originally joined because I couldn't play netball anymore due to a ruptured tendon in my finger, and I needed to do something for myself. I've always loved music. Mum and Dad used to run Square Dance clubs and my dad was a Square Dance caller. He travelled all over this country and even to America doing it. He would stand on the stage and sing as well as play the records. One thing I wish I had been made to do when I was little is to play the piano. Instead, I played the viola. I have no idea why. I probably showed aptitude in a music test and the school needed a viola player! I still think that maybe one day I will learn the piano, it's never too late. I love music, and always have headphones on even when I'm at work.

A little while ago, we had the opportunity of going to Barcelona with Rock Choir to perform at various locations. This gave me the kick start I needed to lose some weight and I felt that was the ideal time to do something about it. I've battled forever with my weight, probably since I was about twenty-two and have never been a little person. I've always been sporty and played a lot of netball from leaving school up until I was about forty-five.

One of my friends, Sally, is a Cambridge Diet Consultant. My head was in the right place and I had a purpose: I had about five months until the Barcelona trip so I knew whatever I did had to be fairly radical and quick! I always believed I carried the extra weight quite well but now when I look back at photographs perhaps I didn't! I knew that I had to get serious and if I didn't do this by myself, I wouldn't do it at all. It was then that I approached Sally and started my Cambridge journey with just shakes and bars for four months.

I had lost about three stone by the time we went to Barcelona, which was enough to make me realise I could do this and more things could potentially happen in life. My confidence was beginning to grow. Altogether now I've lost five stone. I have managed to maintain my weight loss, but I did put on a stone last Christmas, so went on one of these six-week high intensity training programmes and managed to lose it. Cambridge is tough and hard and if I went back to what I ate before, the weight would all go back on. There is a reason I was seventeen stone and the reason was I ate too much food. I am of an age now where if I go out for a meal, I can put on half a stone overnight!

Some people say it is a fad diet, but for me it did what it needed to do. I also realise the importance of exercise and do much more now. My confidence has increased to the point where I am now confident enough to take solos in choir, something I would never have done before. I feel so good when I've done a solo, it is such an achievement and everyone is so supportive. I think if I hadn't lost the weight I would still be hiding away.

Friendships have been an important part of my choir journey. I'd originally joined Rock Choir with my dearest friend Sarah, whom I'd gone to school with. We were both in the bass section, which she found too low so moved to altos. I've known Sue for about thirty years having both worked for the same company and in the same team for a lot of that time and when Sarah left, I persuaded Sue to come along, knowing she enjoyed music and the arts, having been a dancer previously. She didn't take too much persuading and questioned why I hadn't asked her in the first place! Nikki was already in the choir but we hadn't spoken much as she was friendly with another group who subsequently moved to the alto section, leaving her on her own in the bass section, which is when we started chatting. She is such a bad influence on me but I count her as one of my closest friends now. We since found out that we attended the same school although Nikki was about ten years below me. It's lovely that Sarah joined Sweet Charity too, as we are singing together again.

I have never been very good at talking about or selling myself so knowing I wanted to contribute to this book I asked both my daughters what they had noticed since I joined choir, and these are the emails I received:

"Since my mum started in the choir I have noticed a dramatic change in her morale. She's made amazing friends that we now count as family. Her confidence has gone from strength to strength and seeing her sing solo in the middle of Bournemouth town centre made me so proud of how far she has come. The choir has opened up so many doors for her and she has done things and gone places she would never have done before she joined."
Rebecca Fish

"Since my mum became part of a choir it has really changed her life and also ours, she has become much more confident as a person and had the courage to do things I could never have imagined her doing years ago. Her friendships she has gained through choir are also another large aspect, being able to have likeminded people who she not only sees at choir but also meets up with separately. Seeing her confidence change

has not only affected herself but also me and the rest of the family. Being able to watch her perform and say: 'That's my mum' is one of those moments not many people have, but I'm so grateful to be able to do it. Also not to mention the opportunity that being part of a choir has offered her, being able to raise money for charities of their choice, and also the opportunity to perform and not only local performances. Even if it does mean I have to listen to the songs constantly, I am glad she joined the choir."
Emily Fish


I just think Sweet Charity and the opportunity of going to New York is amazing. We get to do things I would never have had the chance to do otherwise. Jenny is inspirational and I have never come across anyone like her before. She can make anybody feel good about themselves and brings out the best in everybody, which must be tough for her. I think there is so much pressure on her. We were singing on the South Bank in London recently and during a break I noticed she was sitting drinking a coffee with a constant stream of people going up to her when I'm sure she just wanted to relax. She's incredible and such a force of nature. During choir sessions there is no time for chit-chat. If someone does start to talk, a glance from Jenny is enough to stop it. The standard is high and we work hard to achieve it.

I do pick and choose when to listen to my choir songs though, as I have to be in the right mood for that. When we all come together and sing in rehearsals you can't think of anything else, you have to clear your mind and concentrate. Nikki is often on call and has to check her phone and send messages to work and I honestly don't know how she concentrates. If I drift for a second, I wonder what I have missed. Music is really important, it's good for the soul and makes you feel good. I think as we go through life we are always finding new songs to love, and this includes in choir. There are songs I never knew before we started learning them, and some if I am honest that I am wary of, but I know how talented Jenny is. She knows exactly what she is doing and I trust her completely.

Morbid as it sounds, I have chosen my funeral songs: Ellie Goulding's "How Long Will I Love You" and Aretha Franklin's "Say A Little Prayer". I was sitting in the car once with my Mum listening to an Adele song which she loved and said she wanted playing at her funeral, so we did just that. It felt good honouring her request and I think it is really important when you are saying your last goodbye to someone to use a piece of music that holds great meaning for them personally.

Sandra Fish
Customer Relations Technician

* * *

At the point when Sweet Charity started, I was in a really bad place in respect of my mental health. Things first started to change for me when I was nine or ten years old. My grandmother was diagnosed with a brain tumour and from that point on, I started controlling food and had eating disorders from the latter part of primary school and into secondary school. I would go all day without eating at school, having thrown my packed lunch away, and I wouldn't eat in front of people. After school, I would binge and then make myself sick and as things progressed, I began to take laxatives as well. I knew this wasn't right, but didn't have a name for it. I was bullied a bit but would clown around and laugh things off, hiding my feelings well, but it really hurt and my self esteem was damaged badly. I eventually confided in a friend whose stepdad was a paramedic. She invited me to her house after school and, unbeknown to me, she and her stepdad had arranged for a friend of theirs, who was a nurse, to be there as well and talk to me. Off the back of that, I confided in my brother who is a little bit older and asked him to tell my parents because I just couldn't.

I was fourteen by this time and my Mum took me to the doctor, who promptly put me on the scales and told me that yes I was a little bit overweight, the worst thing she could possibly have said. She referred me to a counsellor who to me, at that age, looked about

42

one hundred and ten years old and proceeded to tell me that it was very fashionable to have bulimia because of Princess Diana. I just shut my mouth at that point and felt unable to say anything else. It made me feel awful. Funnily enough, a couple of years ago I was receiving some counselling and this experience just popped into my mind after not talking about it at all for all those years. I felt so angry towards this guy. I was ready to put in a formal complaint, but although my present counsellor confirmed that what he had said was highly inappropriate, she was hesitant about what could be done or achieved if I did make that complaint, so I left it. I think talking about it and having it acknowledged helped a lot.

I suppose bulimia was still quite misunderstood in the mid-nineties and the fact the doctor had put me on the scales was so wrong. It's nothing to do with weight, it is a mental health issue linked to control. After that traumatic experience I pretended to my parents that I was fine and hid everything from them. I kept all my feelings buried deeply.

Up until I was about seventeen, I was actively bulimic and didn't say a word to anyone. I have never coped well with change and each time there was a transition in my life, the feeling of needing to regain control would come back strongly. Going to college was another trigger point and, in the January after I started, I was constantly binging, purging and starving, in this whole cycle of behaviour. I wasn't talking to anyone and felt increasingly low. In the February I took an overdose, which I guess was a cry for help and brought things to a head. My mum came upstairs that night to have a chat with me and I explained to her that things had got bad again. At the end of the conversation, I blurted out to her that I had taken some tablets about an hour previously. Of course, my parents rushed me straight to A&E where I had my stomach pumped, which was pretty traumatic. After that I got some proper help, saw a really good counsellor and was put on antidepressants. I'm not sure how much that helped, as I felt a little bit dependent on it and consequently if I forgot to take it, I would flip out. I still wasn't in a good way and certainly not at ease with the fact I was on antidepressants, as there was still quite a stigma at that point.

Going to university in London was another big change for me. I'd been with my boyfriend, now my husband, since we were sixteen and it was difficult, as he was still living in our home town of Andover. I was really unhappy to start with, but we saw each other most weekends. About half way through my first year I went to see a homeopath that my mum's friend had recommended and after an indepth consultation she gave me a remedy. I only saw her once but I was able to come off Prozac just like that. Of course, that wouldn't work for everybody, but for me it really helped. I felt euphoric and it had a really big impact on me. I was fine for a period of about 8 or 9 months after that, but then the winter drew in and I started slipping again. I went to a doctor in London who diagnosed me with Seasonal Affective Disorder (SAD). So there I was, diagnosed with depression, bulimia, traits of anorexia and now SAD. I was put on some different antidepressants, and I got a light box to try light therapy - basically just trying the best I could to get on with life at uni. Each time winter came around, I would take a dip again. During my second year, I really was quite low and struggled to leave the house, or if I did it would be to just disappear. I would often go into London on my own, wander around and be totally anonymous. It was a total escape. I even get that now where I want to go where nobody knows me, be anonymous and disappear. I'm proud to say I completed my course and graduated from university, although it certainly wasn't always easy.

After uni, I lived at home for a year and was feeling better than I had been for a while. I had learned to recognise my signals by then, so knew when I was taking a bit of a dip. October and November were always tricky months and I would have to keep an eye on myself. I was working at a school by then, which really helped as I had a certain responsibility and there were people who needed me to be okay. I couldn't just give in to it. I'm a Capricorn and take my responsibilities seriously!

I had every intention to train as a teacher but it didn't work out and I quit halfway through. Looking back, I think it was anxiety that made me stop. It was another change for me. I had been on one placement and I was about to go to a girls' grammar school. I was convinced they were going to find me out and know I wasn't good enough. That has been a recurrent theme playing in my mind.

My husband had moved down to Bournemouth whilst I was at uni, so we decided to move in together during this time. I now had a job at a SEN school, working with people with learning difficulties. My mid-twenties were pretty good and I was quite stable. I felt I was good at my job, I had more confidence and I was well respected at work. I would say that was probably the best period of my life.

Aged twenty-six, we were approached to see if we would consider fostering my nephews and we were twenty-seven when they moved in with us, aged twelve and seven. We have an amazing relationship with the older one now but at the time, we couldn't give him what he needed so he went elsewhere but our youngest nephew was with us for ten years up until last year.

While he was with us, we went on to have our own children. My daughter was born in 2009 and unfortunately, I had a really traumatic birth, ending with a general anaesthetic to get her out quickly. It was all so quick and my husband wasn't allowed to stay with me. I knew it had affected me a little bit but didn't realise the full extent. I thought I had let my daughter down, that my body had let her down, that I had let my husband down because he couldn't be there. I felt like a complete failure. Yet again I buried all these feelings and emotions thinking I wasn't able to talk about it. Because of my history of depression, I thought I may be more susceptible to post-natal depression. However, what I was experiencing wasn't depression and the questions they asked me to try and ascertain if I was depressed were not revealing anything. Something wasn't right but I wasn't aware of what it was so I just got on with things because that's what we all do.

When my daughter was about two, I joined Jenny's Christchurch Rock Choir after meeting a friend who was already a member, and absolutely loved it from the day I started. I'd sung at school and college and took my degree in drama but always wanted to be in a choir. Like most people I would sing in the shower or the car on my own but the opportunity had never presented itself before and other things would take over. This was now something I enjoyed and, more importantly, something for me. Within the first term we were learning 'Don't let the sun go down on me' and not knowing any better I volunteered for the solo part. I did receive a very good response and ended up singing that solo in Christchurch Priory at one of our concerts. It was such a boost for me and I absolutely loved that feeling.

Not long after, I found I was pregnant with my son. This time my pregnancy was more challenging. Within the first week of finding out I was pregnant I was bleeding. The doctor told me to go home and the pain would get worse and it would probably 'pass through'. That was obviously upsetting, but I accepted that, as I knew that about one in four recognised pregnancies end in a miscarriage. I went home and nothing happened apart from intermittent bleeding. I managed to make it through to eleven weeks when they could finally scan me and everything was fine. Unfortunately though, I was found to have gestational diabetes. The bleeding was never explained and it continued so there was a lot going on, and I underwent a lot of checks throughout the whole pregnancy.

Contractions started at about twenty-nine weeks. I was admitted into hospital where they put me on a monitor, but everything had stopped by then and they were on the point of sending me home when the machine suddenly went crazy. I can't remember the name of the test they gave me next but it can detect if you are likely to go into labour. I showed positive which meant I was likely to although it wasn't definite. I was then in hospital for a few days on different drugs to try and halt the labour. They sent me home hoping I could get to thirty-six weeks. In the end, he was born at thirty-eight weeks and five days. For that whole period of uncertainty, we didn't go anywhere we didn't do anything. I think that is when my anxiety started, although I didn't have a name for it, I just knew things were not good. It started with me feeling a little bit low again.

I had a natural birth, which I had been hoping for as I was desperate to do it 'right' this time. While that was lovely and a huge relief, it reinforced all the feelings I'd had about Tilly's birth and I asked myself "why couldn't I have done it right for her?". I had two small children and my nephew was a teenager, who had just started secondary school. All these things combined and one day I was out with the children and just felt completely out of my depth. I had an overwhelming feeling that I couldn't keep them safe. I felt as if I wasn't good enough as a mum, which was ridiculous as I'd been a foster mum for ages and I'd had regular assessments by social workers. With my own kids though, I felt I was failing, although I didn't voice any of it. When anyone else was with me I was putting on this brave face and I think that in itself was part of the problem. It was all an act and I was telling everyone I was fine.

A year later my daughter was due to start school, another change of course. I really dipped at this point and felt things were spiralling out of control. It was different this time, which I now know was anxiety. On the back of this I started feeling very low indeed. I stopped doing things I enjoyed and avoided going out. If I had both of the kids and my husband wasn't there, I would struggle even going to the park with them. Horrible scenarios would run through my head and would play out like a film. For example, I would see us doing the school run and I would see as clear as day in my head a bus plough into us on the pavement and all the carnage that followed. This had such a detrimental effect on my life and I had to do something as I felt like I was going mad, so I went back to a homeopath. I was worried and had no idea what was wrong with me.

She talked to me about absolutely everything ranging from food cravings to sleep patterns and then to the birth of my kids, which is when the floodgates opened and it all poured out of me. For the very first time, someone acknowledged that I had experienced birth trauma. This was actually a thing with a name that can have a huge impact on your life, and here was someone empathising and understanding how I was feeling. I went to her for two years and it certainly helped to a point. She told me it was like treating two people because I would either go along and be really anxious and unable to go out, which she would then treat and the anxiety would lift but I would then slip into depression and she would have to lift me up from that. They were both as debilitating as each other, but with the anxiety my brain never stopped and I had this constant noise in my head saying "What if? What if? What if?" So many scenarios playing out in my mind so clearly, it was really disturbing. It was when I slipped into depression that the thoughts got really dark. For two years, I was just going through the motions of daily life and doing the bare minimum.

The school run became a huge struggle, because my son was wanting to be out of his push chair more and more. It probably sounds really stupid but he was into everything and I just saw danger everywhere and was constantly risk-assessing. I would get home from school and dissolve into floods of tears. Most of my anxiety was around my kids and keeping them safe and I would avoid certain places or situations as I didn't believe I was capable of keeping them safe, I wasn't good enough. Of course, I couldn't stay in forever and I did have some pretty massive panic attacks on occasions whilst I was out. It was also putting a huge amount of pressure on my relationship with my husband, who found it difficult to understand what was happening to me.

It became apparent to me that I needed more help than the homeopath could give. I think because I was fostering, it had always been at the back of my mind that I couldn't ask for help with my mental health as it would go on to my record and might work against me, although that was probably anxiety itself.

It was beginning to creep into other areas of my life, as I hadn't been attending Rock Choir. I was struggling to get there. My mum would come along to babysit and I'd leave the house but then just drive somewhere and sit in the car. I just couldn't get through the door. Around then Jenny held a workshop with the Lounge Kittens to learn 'Africa', which I really wanted to do, so I signed up for it. This was a huge deal for me as I wasn't in a good place. During the break Jenny asked me a question and I just crumbled and fell apart. Jenny was wonderful and just stroked my hand but I felt like I didn't want to live any more, it was pretty dark. Of course, Jenny and Kym, my friend at choir, had no idea I had been going through all this and it was the first time I had said anything to anyone other than the homeopath. This made me realise I could talk to people about it, including my husband. Soon after this, Jenny announced she was starting up Sweet Charity, and I knew I had to go and that it would be good for me.

I remember someone in the choir, whom I had been Facebook friends with for a while, posted something about the struggles they had been through and how they had coped, so the next time I saw them I blurted some stuff out and they mentioned the various avenues of help they had tried and how positive it had been for them. From that and with the support of some close friends and family, I plucked up the courage to go to the doctor and poured everything out. I had more counselling and some CBT and I also saw someone privately who specialises in birth trauma and uses a hypnotherapy technique of re-programming your mind to think differently about the birth. I now feel completely different about my daughter's birth, and can think about it without crying. I was also given some antidepressants, which I am still on to this day. They help with anxiety as well, and has stopped all the 'noise' in my head which means I can enjoy life now.

In Sweet Charity we have time to chat, drink tea and eat cake. I have made such amazing friends whom I can talk to, who know who I am and to whom I can say anything. When we did the recording for 'Come Alive', I got incredibly emotional that day. I was singing that song with those lyrics: "You saved me the day you came alive" and it really resonated with me. I realised as I sang it that is exactly how I felt in that moment about the choir. I had tears falling down my face. Jenny's arrangements are so beautiful, she draws the best from people and musically it just does something to me. Some people don't understand why I cry in choir, but it can just be a couple of notes or a particular lyric and I'm gone. The songs can be so challenging and you can escape into a different world of concentrating and learning with no time to think of anything else. The friendships, the fun and the opportunities are incredible, and of course I cannot wait for New York, I still can't quite believe it! Just knowing I have the support of choir once a month helps me so much. It's part of my self-care now and, whilst I still have bad days,

I am so much better than I was. Sweet Charity was a real turning point for me and that choir literally saved my life.

Becky Guest
Autism Support Worker

\* \* \*

Music has really helped with my confidence. I had always wanted to join a choir and I first joined one of Jenny's Rock Choirs in Christchurch, Dorset in 2013 which was an amazing experience and I made some very close friendships, which I've kept to this day. Like many others, I followed Jenny to Sweet Charity. When you are with like-minded people, especially with singing, you form a close bond and of course we have so much fun and a real laugh as well.

When Sweet Charity recorded 'Come Alive', the whole experience was extremely emotional and enabled me to open up to Jenny about a very painful time in my life which I had so far kept quite private. My dad had battled for many years with a severe and deep depression, which got worse every winter, and this in turn eventually led to him committing suicide in 1987. Although it doesn't seem that long ago, it was like a different world at that time. Dad was a successful local photographer and although he had suffered for ten years, his condition hadn't even been diagnosed with a particular name, although I believe he was bipolar. He was on medication, but there was little or no additional support, and I mean nothing. No counselling, no group therapy sessions, in fact no one even spoke about it back then. This was 1987, not Victorian times! As a family, we were at a complete loss as to what to do and totally ill-equipped as to how to deal with or help Dad with his illness.

I was 24 when I heard the news of his death and I was living in Canada with my husband, who was working there at the time. My mum was also with us. Dad had organised for her to come out to stay with us for a holiday and it was my sister who found him. It was an extremely traumatic time.

When we sang and recorded 'Come Alive' it was an incredibly powerful experience but I really held my emotions together for the whole process. I thought it was a wonderful thing that Jenny was doing and I have always admired how open and honest she is with her own mental health. Everything about this song and what we did had a real impact on me, and reading some of the comments people put on YouTube made me realise how people can now talk and share how they feel, something my dad had never had. Even his closest friends were not aware of his illness. There is such a huge difference between now and then, when no one spoke about, let alone admitted to having, mental health issues in whatever form. It makes me very sad to think that Dad didn't have the support and help that is available now. So, when I read those comments on YouTube, I suddenly felt very honoured to be part of such an amazing choir, doing something so unique.

Six months later, long after the initial reaction and euphoria following the video had died down, I felt I really wanted Jenny to know how I felt and how personal this was to me. I didn't want to say anything at the time as everyone seemed so happy but I needed her to know how special her idea was, to spread this message of sharing and honesty. In the end I poured all my thoughts and feelings into an email to Jenny, which was therapeutic in itself, and of course she was lovely as always. I felt so grateful that I could open up at last. I still don't tell that many people. The way Dad died was horrific, but I do believe in many ways there is a lot more hope out there and I am so glad about that. I feel so honoured to be part of something with people who are willing to share their experiences.

Of course, the other benefit of singing in a choir is learning the lyrics. It's a great brain workout and definitely one of the best things for me. There are many things I can't do but the lyrics stay in my mind! When I've cracked those lyrics I really feel like I've achieved something. It's difficult to explain the joy and feeling that choir provides. The emotion it generates can take me by surprise and I find I well up sometimes even during the warm ups and I could easily cry. I feel such a sense of pride in such a beautiful sound that we make. I just love every minute of choir, it is such an uplifting experience and I would recommend it to anyone.

Kym Mason
Retired Medical Laboratory Assistant

**Choir And Cake**

Many years ago I joined Rock Choir. I enjoyed singing and thought it would be a nice way to meet new people.

That first day I walked into the school hall and was greeted by a young woman who was very friendly and encouraging. She introduced herself as 'Jenny'. A lady called Di said simply to me, "It's wonderful. You'll love it!"

I sat in the Bass harmony section and we sang 'How Deep is Your Love' which was one of my favourites.

I felt back then the learning process was like brain training. You have to re-organise already embedded songs into new harmonies, and remember them. It was nice to be part of a team and sing together. My choir life had begun.

I made the journey every week doing my utmost to make sure Monday evenings were kept free. I didn't want to miss a single session. Not only were the songs fun to learn, and the like-minded people friendly, Jenny, our adored Choir Leader, was a little gem. A powerhouse of activity, full of energy, encouragement, fun, and she made each and every member feel like they were important.

Then, sadly, I was diagnosed with Hodgkins Lymphoma and needed chemotherapy. This was a very negative time of my life. Chemo is a necessary but ruthless treatment, killing not only the nasty cancer cells, but also good cells. Following my treatment my recovery was slow, but I always felt comfort stepping through the door and being enveloped by caring, friendly people. They didn't even seem to mind that I was bald!

Unfortunately, I relapsed about a year later and needed further treatment, much more intensive and scary. The choir members were there for me, understanding, empathetic and helpful. They brought me meals after I had been discharged from hospital, drove me to appointments, kept in touch, bought gifts, entertained me and I'm sure lots of other things my chemo brain has packed neatly away in my head.

Chemo left me with quite a few issues: heart failure, shortness of breath, peripheral neuropathy, muscle and bone pain, digestive problems, loss of memory, anxiety and low self-esteem, to name just a few. Luckily my hair grew back!!

Singing has helped tremendously. My lung capacity has improved much faster than expected. My anxiety is non-existent when I'm at choir, and I'm sure learning all these songs has helped with my memory, although I still forget what I'm looking for when I go into a room for something, and I still put the coffee pot in the fridge and the milk in the washing machine!

Although I'm still with Rock Choir I followed Jenny when she started up Sweet Charity Choir and it has made me feel I am a member of a family. My organisation skills have returned and my self-esteem has been raised. I'm a useful member of a group of friends ... I get to sing ... and what's more I get to eat cake! The cake is wonderful! As I've said so many times, Jenny should be available on prescription on the NHS!

I get to perform in amazing places. I help to fund raise for charity. I laugh. I push myself and am pushed (musically of course) by Jenny. I sing the most wonderful songs arranged by a skilful musician whom I class as a friend, a pocket rocket who has charm, humour, care, and sensitivity, whom I respect, and I'm in awe of her musical ability and her achievements.

Thank goodness for Sweet Charity Choir, and Jenny D.

Jilly Firmin
Personal Assistant/ Author/Single Mum

* * *

I never had any plans to sing in a choir, although I have sung many times before. In fact, I was a boy soprano in my school choir and I also played trombone in a band. We even made a record, which was recorded in the school hall one Sunday afternoon. My name appears on the album credits more than anyone else's, as a member of the choir, a soloist singing 'Once in Royal David's City', and the trombonist. My voice was just on the point of breaking, so we had about ten takes to get one good one. Music is a massive part of me. I don't have particular favourites though, and tend to go through phases that sometimes change daily, listening to anything from Pink Floyd, Nirvana and Foo Fighters, to Craig David, Bruno Mars and Nina Simone, depending on my mood. My guilty secret at the moment is Harry Styles - his latest solo album is fantastic and I play it endlessly. I also enjoy classical music and those who know me know you can't get me off karaoke, which I absolutely love. I also love my sport and I play golf and go bowling, and I'm a massive Leicester City fan, so one of the greatest moments of my life was when they won the league a couple of years ago.

It was Annie, my wife, who originally dragged me along kicking and screaming to join Rock Choir. I really didn't want to go. After that first session I came away thinking "No, that's not for me". Annie persuaded me to give it one more go and the rest is history. I was in Rock Choir for eight years and a 'prefect' for seven of them. I'm the sort of person who doesn't do things by halves, it's not in my nature. I'm either all in or not in at all so I really threw myself into it.

After Jenny left it got to a point quite quickly where for me it was all about the people, more so than the singing. Being a Rock Choir 'prefect' meant I was the one greeting people, having a bit of a laugh, being cheeky and I really thrived on that. Once I'd signed everyone in I could have gone home because the singing side of it wasn't really doing it for me.

I suspect I'm not the only one, but choir for me is really all about Jenny. Life is never a smooth journey for any of us and she's been there lots of times for me over the years and I'd like to think I have for her as well. People would be surprised if they knew about me because the 'me' that is out there is this larger than life character who is the life and soul of the party, whereas underneath all that bravado is just 'bits' and the bravado is just a coping mechanism. I sometimes feel like I'm performing. I think depression has always been there and I've been fighting it for most of my life but I just never realised it. I found it so easy to get totally entrenched in my coping mechanisms and the lines have become blurred between the reality and what I am doing to cope. I spent years and years, and still do now, asking myself just who I am. Am I the Colin who people would identify with here, or am I the depressed Colin with low self-confidence? I really don't know sometimes.

I've been to the doctor's countless times over the years and received various types of counselling and medication but despite that I've hit rock bottom on three occasions. Each time I've reached that desperate point and decided on what it is I'm going to do, I find a strength, something deep within that pulls me back from the edge and it's then that I allow myself to completely break down. It's almost like a reset button. If I'm being cynical it's when I reach that point that people seem to spring into life and appear from nowhere with all the offers of support and I think well hold on, there are times leading up to this that I have tried to talk to people but no one wants to get involved. It's easy for people to say those things like 'let me know if I can help', or 'I'm here if you want to talk', especially after the event, but if two days ago I had tried to talk to them they would probably have said, "Oh you'll be alright, don't worry", when actually, no, I clearly wasn't going to be alright. I know that logically it's easier to talk to a stranger and of course I know people care about me, but when I am going through the really dark times I just think that no one cares and the world wouldn't stop turning if I wasn't here anymore. I've done some stupid things in my life and I'm not necessarily an easy person to get on with or live with. I do things that leave me cringing after which I could absolutely beat myself up and send myself through the floor, and which can take me weeks to get over.

People often say that I'm a nice bloke and I'd do anything for anyone but I have this constant battle in my mind questioning if that is true, or if I am just being nice to gain approval and receive the feedback that I need. I'll tie myself in knots and from that it is so easy to spiral downwards, which I've done so many times. I have this deep-rooted need to be loved and appreciated but in seeking that, the reality of who I am becomes blurred. I've sat in therapy and actually said to the therapist that I don't know which of these people is really me. The reply was not to put myself in a box as I'm probably a bit of all of it.

I come from a working-class background, but I was a bit of a child prodigy and the most intelligent kid in the school. Of course there hadn't been anyone in the family like this before and they didn't understand how to deal with me. As a result it led to this expectation of perfection all the time. Whether it was the underlying pressure or the boredom of the majority of my school life that triggered my mental health issues I don't know. We would be taught something at school which I grasped straight away and then spend another fortnight on it for the others to learn it. It became expected for me to get top marks and if I got a 'B' my parents would wonder what I'd been up to. I don't blame them for that, they knew no different and I've convinced myself they were trying to do the best for me, but I always felt like I was a disappointment. Initially I became a bit of a class clown, like I am now really, but then I went off the rails and started to rebel. As an adult looking back I think, "what a prat!". I could have been anything I wanted to be, but I left school and worked in a butchers. Through all the therapies I've had, a lot of my self-confidence issues and approval seeking comes back to that.

Choir gives me a sense of purpose that I need and find it difficult when I don't have that purpose. If I give myself time to think, my thoughts are generally negative, so I keep as busy as I can. I hate my job with a vengeance and have a lot of problems there, but I'm hoping for early retirement and to do something I do like to top up my income, which no doubt will help me feel much better. I've started my own business making pens and have set up a workshop in my garage. As I've said before I have two speeds, full speed ahead and dead stop, so within a week I had bought a domain, created a website and already I'm planning to do craft shows to sell my pens.

It's only in the last four or five years where I have felt comfortable talking about my issues. Prior to that it felt like a sign of weakness and I would have been mortified for people to know I was going through such things. Men do find it very difficult to open up, but hopefully that is all changing now. Coming to choir, and particularly Sweet Charity, plays a big part in keeping me on the good side of things. It's not just the singing, although the enjoyment of that has come back to me now, but being part of this choir family gives me a sense of belonging. I come through the door and receive hug after hug after hug, there is just so much love in the room. I've come to choir on days where I feel in a really bad place and gone home feeling so much better, and a lot of that for me is the interaction with the people here. I don't consider myself to be anyone special within the choir but everyone knows me. I agree with others who say it is a safe place to be, it's totally non-threatening. I mean where else would you get such amazing opportunities as singing in Carnegie Hall in New York? It's mental! When I tell people what I'm doing and that it is just us appearing there, they genuinely can't believe it! As well as seeing family whilst we're there, we've got tickets for the baseball, which I'm really looking forward to.

For years and years, I've created this false persona of this larger than life character and haven't allowed myself to show any weakness, but now finally I have got to a point in my life where I can say, here I am, yes I am flaky, but this is how I am, and this is what I am. If there is one thing to take away from this that I would really like to get across, is when you see someone who appears to have it all together, and they appear really confident, just try to look beyond that and dig a bit deeper and have a chat. They could just be putting on a brave face too. It is a constant daily struggle for some of us. In all my bravado, I sometimes overstep the mark and then cringe, beat myself up and want to disappear. Don't always believe what you see or what people are portraying.

Colin Fleming
Data Management Lead

57

## Power of Music

It's difficult to know where to start. We all carry 'baggage' through our lives which, along with the day to day challenges we face, helps mould us into the people we are today. I certainly carry more than my fair share of baggage from my past and have had a lot to deal with over the years from an early age and though I have been low many times have always seemed to bounce back.

Leading up to and eventually separating from my wife was a particularly difficult time, and I was having suicidal thoughts. Music helped get me through that time and although it didn't stop those thoughts it became in some ways like an addictive drug.

When Jen left Rock Choir to pursue other musical aspirations it coincided with me experiencing really low self-esteem issues relating to my realisation that I was not the greatest of singers which in turn made me feel depressed. I continued with Rock Choir for a while and managed to hide my feelings behind the mask we all wear in public, but it all proved too much for me and I soon left.

Just before Sweet Charity started, Jen held a "Sing Like a Kitten" workshop with the Lounge Kittens, with the idea of learning one of their arrangements. I hadn't been singing for a while and I hesitated before deciding to attend. I thought it would be a good opportunity to see if I was up to singing with a group again with the possibility of going back to Rock Choir. I emailed Jen beforehand explaining my problems. She said there would be people there that I knew and I could do as much or as little as I felt able to. The lead up to the day was hard as I was getting more and more anxious and wasn't sure if I would cope.

On the day itself I drove to the school and sat in the car park for a while, wrestling internally with myself as to whether or not I should go in. I almost decided against it but I saw some familiar faces which was reassuring, so summoning up my courage I decided to face my demons. I went in and signed in at the desk with Zan and Timia (the other two Kittens). Zan said how lovely it was to see me and it was great I had managed to come along and I think they said they were proud of me having taken such a big step. I was so completely overwhelmed with the kind words and friendly faces that I couldn't hold it together anymore and dashed out into the corridor where I broke down in tears. I was distraught.

Jen came out to comfort me and gently coaxed me into going back into the hall. I remember telling her I would try to hold it together.

In the event I got through the session with no problems. As we went along with the music I relaxed and any thoughts of low self-esteem seemed to wash away. I didn't crack and I felt my anxiousness had subsided as I experienced that feel-food factor of singing together again with a group of people creating a harmonious sound. At the end Jen said that she had noticed I did fine and she could hear me! (Not sure if that was a good thing!)

I returned to Rock Choir shortly after for a while but still found it difficult as my self-esteem issues continued. I'd heard about Sweet Charity starting up but at first didn't think it was for me, so missed some of the earlier sessions. I thought perhaps private singing lessons might help. I asked my teacher what she thought of my voice as I wanted to know what was a comfortable range for me so I could gauge where to pitch my voice, and I needed her to be honest and truthful. She didn't say my voice was great – but that it was not bad and I had a pretty good range. This helped but I wasn't convinced!

After a few months of lessons, I decided to give Sweet Charity a go, as there were a lot of people there that I knew. My self-esteem has definitely improved although I do still have issues and I guess like many other people I'm probably my own most critical judge.

There is something slightly mystical about singing as a group and I feel an invisible support connecting us as we sing. Sometimes, even during the most challenging songs, I experience a release of endorphins which makes me feel good at the end of the session, and of course Jen makes it fun and entertaining even when she works us hard.

At the beginning I said music was like a drug and addictive and I believe that, as you experience a natural high. As well as being a mass of like-minded people wanting to sing and make great sounds together, the choir is a family who look out for and support each other physically, mentally and possibly unknowingly, spiritually, and we all come together to get that fix to help us through the weeks.

Nick McCullen (aka Mr Nick)
Engineer

* * *

I belong to the Verwood Choir, having joined at the start. I would never have thought I would be in a Choir, so it is a complete surprise and joy to me that here I am, singing and loving being in one.

Jenny is such a huge inspiration, she makes it fun, but also expects a high professional standard from us. Her harmonies are just beautiful, and I just enjoy hearing the songs when we have learnt them, and the melodies that merge together so creatively. Wow, that was Us!

I have made new friends, and feel very much part of the Choir family. There is a bond growing between us as we go on our musical journey. Some of us have not been in Choirs before, so our mutual support and feeling of achievement are very genuine.

I do like the aspect that we also support Charities every time we meet. So not only do we have a very enjoyable afternoon, with delicious cake, we are also helping others who are in need of help.

It is a huge privilege to be performing at Carnegie Hall, a real opportunity of a lifetime, and it just shows you never quite know what is round the corner.

Jane Forrest

* * *

I sadly divorced a long time ago and during that dark period, in addition to bringing up my children without a partner, I also had to deal with bowel cancer and the death of both my father and my mother. None of those things are easy when you're on your own. I don't really want to go into any of it too deeply as I'm sure there are an awful lot of other people in similar positions, however I did have times of wondering if this was really all life had to offer. I felt like I was doing nothing just for me.

Then, one Christmas, I was watching Gareth Malone on television doing the first of the Military Wives Choirs episodes. I sat there fascinated and experienced what I can only assume was an epiphany. Although I used to sing at school, I had no idea if I could still sing or not. That didn't matter though, I just knew I had to find a choir. I didn't tell anybody of my plan at first as I had a feeling people would try and put me off or want to come with me and I needed to do something on my own.

And so it was that I joined New Forest Rock Choir in what I think was Jenny's second year, which was being held at the time in Brockenhurst Village Hall, a stone's throw from where I lived. I walked into that hall on my very first session and I think I was the first to arrive. Jenny greeted me with that beautiful smiley face of hers. I didn't mention the doubts I had about singing. Just nervously told her I had joined as a 'tastee'. She immediately put me at ease, telling me there were a few new members that night and directed me over to what I now know was the bass section. I'd forgotten at that point how choirs work and it turns out that was right for my voice, however I remember there were only about six of us in that section and I think she was putting all of us new people in the basses!

I loved every moment of Rock Choir with Jenny, I had never known anyone who was so inspirational and motivated. Like everyone else in RC, I had a really big wobble when Jenny left to pursue her dream with the Lounge Kittens. I was so happy when she came back into my life and Sweet Charity was formed and of course I absolutely love it. I love the surprises and opportunities Jenny gives us along with everything else; the friendship, the feeling of belonging and of course the cakes! I really don't know how she'll top New York, but knowing Jenny she'll have something planned! I love Jenny, she is so extraordinarily talented that sometimes I forget to sing, I am so in awe of her; I literally just find myself watching how she conducts everyone, how she can hear one wrong note, encourage us and play so beautifully. She really is quite amazing.

I feel I have changed so much since joining choir and I've made so many new friends during these past six years. I have even met one lady who I went to school with and we hadn't seen each other since that time. Friends and family comment how they have never seen me the way I am now. Previously I used to dread weekends and could sometimes go through the entire weekend without speaking to anybody. My children are grown up now and doing their own thing so I certainly didn't want to impose on them, and got into the habit of allowing work to fulfil me.

I think my crowning glory was last Christmas when my daughter came to our concert at Verwood. She was absolutely blown away by our performance. I was with her on Christmas Day and happened upon her playing a video of us to her friend. I retreated back into the hall and heard her saying, "Look there's my mum. Aren't they amazing?" I felt very proud indeed. I can safely say that choir has absolutely saved me as a person.

Christine Hensser
Bookkeeper

**Finding My Voice**

My mother always told me I was tone deaf. I believed her and so didn't sing because she always told me my voice was terrible. I never auditioned for the school choir or anything else remotely to do with music because she had instilled in me that I couldn't sing and told me "nobody wants to hear that dreadful racket."

And so I listened to music but never sang along out loud, unless I was completely on my own: in the car, in the middle of a field walking the dog – even in the shower! I knew I had a love of singing; silent singing in my head, miming the words.

Then I heard from a friend about a new choir just starting up in Southend. Sweet Charity Choir. There were no auditions, no one would laugh at me or put their hands over their ears. I could maybe get away with it, singing quietly and merging in.

Well, that didn't work. Once I met the inspirational Jenny Deacon and everyone at Sweet Charity Choir that was it. No more silent singing: I found my voice, loud and proud!

Jenny encourages you to do your best. She teaches you how to sing the notes and the words and when and where to breathe. In the year I've been singing with the choir I have gained so much confidence, I've finally found my mojo – I CAN sing!

But I found that singing with other people makes me very emotional, and I have to keep my feelings in check. I have a family member struggling continuously with manic depression and bi polar and the first time we started to sing Jenny's arrangement of the Foo Fighters' 'Come Alive', I wept, really wept. But being surrounded by all my new friends it felt cathartic, good for the soul. I didn't care. Afterwards the choir members hugged me, wiped my tears, and told me they understood. Jenny always says we are part of a big family. The Sweet Charity Family. I feel I really belong.

Singing with Sweet Charity has become the highlight of my week, my "fix". It's my time to shine away from everyday pressures. It's where a bad day can end as a good day; it's where I've made new friends – and even learned how to bake cakes! There is nothing like singing your heart out with friends, seeing them all happy and enjoying the moment.

And now we have the wonderful opportunity to sing in Carnegie Hall, New York! What a fantastic experience that will be. My confidence has grown so much I have volunteered to share a room for four nights with a woman I had never even met, before joining the choir!

The New York trip will be many things: exhilarating, invigorating and emotional, but above all it will forge friendships and camaraderie. The united love of singing will enhance the brotherhood of Sweet Charity Choir, helping it grow stronger and stronger.

Sally Holman
Community Lead for Waitrose and Partners

**Singing Lifts The Spirits**

My twin sister, Rowena, before she died, said, "You should sing, join a choir." After her death that's exactly what I did. She will never know how much this has helped me through difficult times.

Thank you Jenny, and Sweet Charity choir members, for the friendships, support, tears and laughter. Also thank you to Rowena, who gave me the strength and courage to join the Choir.

> "Group singing is cheaper than therapy, healthier than drinking and certainly more fun than working out. It is the one thing in life when feeling better is pretty much guaranteed."
> (Anonymous quote)

Claire Hoyal
Retired Palliative Care Nurse

\* \* \*

In 2012, two days after my fortieth birthday, I walked into a school hall on a Wednesday evening and was greeted by the bright eyes and beaming smile of Jenny Deacon.

A couple of weeks earlier, a friend and colleague had messaged me at work to tell me about a choir she'd recently joined. She knew I loved singing, as some years before with some other friends we'd started our own little barbershop quintet. We never performed outside of our friend's flat, and we only rehearsed a few times, but we enjoyed singing in harmony and sometimes we even sounded quite good when we listened to the taped recording (these were the days before smartphones)!

Some years before that, on a work team-building course, I'd been singing in the minibus on the way to an outdoor adventure. Someone told me that I had a lovely voice. That stuck with me.

I'd never really thought about whether I had a good voice or not, I just sang. A lot. My two sisters and I spent much of our childhood "being" Abba, and we knew all the songs from Joseph and his Amazing Technicolour Dreamcoat. Much to my brother's chagrin, we would perform the entire score on car journeys from East London to Bognor Regis to visit my grandmother. He would take his new-fangled Sony Walkman and listen to Police and Dire Straits while we warbled happily on the back seat of our mum's Ford Escort estate.

In the early noughties, the Singstar game came out on the Playstation. I'd never tried Karaoke in a public place, but found that I could perform with family and friends, and seemed to do rather well – at least, within the fairly limited parameters of Singstar! I'd always fantasised about being a singer (I idolised the Madonna of the "Desperately Seeking Susan" era), but I felt that my nerves would never let me perform in public. I'd always hated being the centre of attention. As soon as eyes were focused on me, I would start to tremble and it would show. People would say, "Oh look, your hands are shaking!" as if I didn't know. So singing would remain a private thing for many years. In the car, in the kitchen while cooking the dinner, in my head...

Then all these choir programmes started popping up on the television (think Gareth Malone), and it was around that time that my friend messaged me. After signing up for a taster session, that evening in April 2012 would change my life. Because whilst singing on my own in front of an audience still strikes the fear of God into me (as does public speaking and making presentations), I found that in the safety of a choir, I could sing out, loud and proud and my voice would hold steady. I had found a way to incorporate singing (and performing) into my life without feeling too exposed.

It helped having Jenny as a leader. Her voice was so pure and clear when demonstrating the harmony parts and her visual cues and gestures made it so easy to pick up both the lyrics and the shape of the harmony. She was awe-inspiring from the start. My first performance with that choir was in the torrential rain in the summer of 2012, for the Olympic torch relay in Southampton. The sound that we made in that rainy park to thousands of people just took my breath away.

But it wasn't just about the singing, it was about the people. As a forty-year old working in a particular type of job for many years, my circle of friends was limited to people like me. Middle class thirty or forty-something graduate professionals working in financial services. Singing in a choir opened up my world to different age-brackets, backgrounds, working environments and world views. I never imagined that I would make a whole new set of friends as I went into my forties, but there is something quite intimate about singing with others that helps to forge new friendships. A shared vulnerability as you learn, but also a shared joy when your voices come together to create an extraordinary wall of sound that can give you goosebumps and bring tears to your eyes. I have laughed and cried with these people at the things we have sung and experienced together.

I have also been more aware of mental health since joining the choir. By meeting new people, particularly younger people who are more aware of and open about their issues, musically talented people who often seem to experience self-doubt and low self-esteem, suddenly, the things you felt and experienced that you thought were just you being a bit weird or a misfit were things that had a name, symptoms of anxiety and depression, things that so many of us feel but never talk about.

I don't often dwell on the sadness that has accompanied me through life. My father dying of cancer when I was just 3 (I don't remember him at all), my mother dying of cancer when I was 27, my own battle with a life-threatening condition at the age of 34. Like everyone, I just carried on, because what is the alternative?

But inevitably, these things have made me who I am today – the apparently strong exterior hiding the quivering mass of nerves underneath. It has made me appreciate the limited time we have on this earth and the importance of spending that time in a way that makes sense and brings joy. For me, singing is a huge part of that. And singing with Jenny Deacon as a leader means that I can be the best that I can be, because of her passion, her precision and her pride in what we as a choir can achieve together.

Susie Withers
Business Analyst

**Rejoice In The Joy**

Singing lifts our hearts
We are there to help and support one another
Everyone is welcome and are
Equally as important
Time flies by when we are together
Charitable donations play a major role for us
Happiness grows alongside our harmonies
All of us value each other and our ethos
Rejoice in the joy of singing
Inspirational sessions by Jenny D are enjoyed and treasured
True friendships have grown
You are never alone being part of the Choir

Anon

**Fate**

How do I feel about your wonderful choir....
I felt sad, disillusioned and had lost my singing mojo...
Then imagine the feeling when you discover a brand new choir, you
join.
Then you realise... it was fate after all, it was meant to be.
A true breath of fresh air, which leaves you with a feel-good factor
every week.

Singing
With Friends Old and New
Energy
Enthusiasm
Tuesdays

Cake
Harmonies
Atmosphere

**R**eal Good Feeling
**I**nspiration
**T**ea Breaks
**Y**ou... Jenny Deacon

Sue Holton

**Finding Myself**

I always thank the day I walked on my own into a choir taught by Jenny.

I was a woman with no confidence or self-belief in any way. I was a bag of nerves at being on my own and facing a challenge for which I was in so many ways totally ill equipped.

Exiting that class was a more confident woman who, with Jenny's continued love and encouragement, has rediscovered her own self.

The music, the singing, the joy of being with such an amazing group of like-minded souls without doubt makes my world a happier and healthier place to be.

Sweet Charity Choir changes many lives.

Thank you Jenny

Dawn Stevens
Retired Personal Assistant

**What Singing And Music Means To Me**

"A world without music would be a very dreary place!"
Moira McGrath

"Joy for the soul"
Jean Cox

"Singing in the choir lifts me up with a great feeling of connection and confidence, it's become an important part of

my life."
Fay Young

"Makes me feel happy and stress free."
Anon

"Music means stepping outside of my life to join a fantastic group of like minded friends to sing in beautiful harmony with each other!
I have never known a release like this and I love it"
Christine Hensser

"Music helps me to express my feelings."
Michael Morgan Age 12

"It has expanded my life in so many ways!"
Sue Everett-Whiten

"An emotional comfort blanket that helps me get through life's ups and downs."
Sue Carter

"Great fun and uplifting. Very satisfying when the songs come together."
Moira McGrath

"Friends and community, creating something together."
Claire Keay

"A pressure valve, to let off steam and forget any stresses."
Sharon Ball

"When singing, the world and its problems are not in the room but outside the door"
Tricia Edwards

"Music is good for my soul. I tie all my memories with certain songs throughout my life."
Lisa Stephens

"Being in a choir helps grow my confidence in singing."
Michael Morgan Age 12

"Lifts my spirits and makes me happy."
Anon

"Lifts my spirits, relaxes me."
Claire Keay

"Absolute freedom."
Dawn Stevens

"It's been lovely meeting new people and singing with the choir really lifts my spirits and makes me happy."
Lisa Stephens

"Lovely meeting new people."
Anon

"Music to me means pure escapism and being in Sweet Charity Choir is like being in a beautiful escape room from which I don't want to escape."
Kym Mason

"Takes you out of yourself."
Anon

"Emotional connection."
Moira McGrath

From members of the Bass section

# It Gives Me Great Pleasure To Present
# The Alto's Anecdotes

## First Choir Performance

First performance in the sweltering heat
It went so well but was quite a feat
I've never perspired as much as today
I'm surprised we didn't all get washed away
Her constant advice, 'Keep yourself hydrated'
As our confidence became elevated
We sang with gusto as the band played loud
And we were all elated, even the crowd
Emotions ran high as we sang our tunes
And our hearts soared like hot air balloons
Unified, together, although clammily
A glorious day spent with my choral family
A special thanks from us all to our lovely Jen
Today I'm free, can we do it again?

Jilly Firmin

## The Soundtrack Of My Life

My depression is a sad song on repeat in my head. The only time the lulling melody lifts is when anxiety decides to play DJ and scratches the sadness into a remix of worry.

Despite this, I still love music.

I was nineteen and away at University when I suffered my first mental breakdown. It was the darkest time of my life. I would go to bed at 8:00 am, sleeping through in order to avoid the guilt of not attending my lectures and waking up to start my 'day' at 10:00 pm. In some ways it was easier to be awake overnight; nobody needed anything from you at 3:00 am. Nobody was around to badger you or chase you for things you have not done because the weight of sadness in your chest was like a hot iron. That was the other problem though, nobody was around.

When I look back on my life during that time and the people I shared it with, we all agree that there was something seriously wrong. I think even now five years on I'm still realising and marvelling at the extent of the psychological damage that period of intense depression and suicidal feeling has had on me. I do not remember November through to March, only a few snippets here and there of clarity and they were not necessarily events I should be proud of.

There is one thing that was constant: Music.

I wrote songs, so many songs. Songs I'll never sing again, songs I cannot even begin to remember. I filled my computer's hard drive with lyrics and melodies and even though I never posted them anywhere I still felt that catharsis.

One afternoon in March towards the end of that brain fog, I stumbled upon a video of my old Rock Choir. It was a video of myself singing a solo at a church, voice blasting up to the literal heavens as a full stage of people I recognised as family sang with me.

I was crying before the opening notes had rung out. I watched the video, remembering who was in the audience to see me that day, the dreams and direction I had had at the time of the performance, the life that I thought I was going to have stretching before me. All of it had gone in the year or so since that video had been filmed, some of it with the click at the end of a phone call, other parts slipping through my fingers like sand.

I wrote a status admitting that I missed it but hoping that it was casual enough to disguise how bereft I was actually feeling. It was suggested that I go back for a visit, and I accepted, hoping the lightness of the offer would never be recognised as the desperate cry for help that it really was.

I went back that week on the Wednesday and that was when everything changed for me.

There is a word; *Sonder:* It is classified as an emotion and used to describe the realisation that the people around you, whether known to you or random, are living their own lives as vivid and complex as your own. I believe that I feel this most when singing with a choir. I stood in that room full of so many different people from all different walks of life and I recognised that the weight of my troubles and the sorrows were probably completely unknown to them all. Though in hindsight that could have made me feel alienated, I felt far from it.

I looked around as we sang, into faces that recognised my pain, smiles that encouraged me to just be in the moment and be together with them. Soon enough I forgot about the darkness, I just let the music and sense of togetherness fill me. It was almost as if I could put down the reins for a while and let my body function on auto-pilot. It was the break and light relief that I needed, a creative outlet and a starting point for a strong support network that has continued to be there for me ever since.

I left university at the end of that year, seeing opportunities for me within my community and music that I had never thought possible before. I got a job at the local hospital and I have risen up the ranks in the IT department, I am the lead singer of two drastically different bands both recording and releasing EPs this year.

I have had therapy for my anxiety and depression and I am looking into getting onto the waiting list for gender identity therapy; something I had not realised was playing such a huge part in my unhappiness until the fog was lifted by meeting other people through music who have struggled with the same thing.

I gained friends and achieved some incredible things with Rock Choir and now with Sweet Charity I find myself looking forward again with the same excitement and lust for life that I had before that darkness took a hold of me.

I know it will come back, the song is never over.
Despite this, I still love music.
Because of music, I still love life.

Beck Lombardi
EPR Product Specialist for the
University Hospital Southampton,
Vocalist & Musician

## The Fabric Of Our Lives

Music, and in particular singing, has always been really important in my family. It is the reason my grandparents and parents met, is a profession for both my sister and cousin, and has been part of the fabric of all of our lives.

Sadly, my mum was diagnosed with terminal cancer in 2015. During her illness, and for some time after her death in July 2016, music was suddenly absent – none of us felt much like singing. I felt very isolated and overwhelmed at that time, feeling a lot of responsibility to make sure everyone else was okay.

After that first Christmas without mum, I was very low, but I thought about the things that were most important to her – singing and charity work – and decided that I wanted to join a choir, in particular one that was socially aware.

That decision led me to the National Health Singers, and through them to Jenny, and through Jenny to Sweet Charity Choir. Singing with such wonderful and generous people, helped me to get through that very difficult time, and has offered me an opportunity to support others.

Jenny and SCC's focus on mental health and music also really spoke to me as I work in mental health services, so have seen the benefit both in my personal and professional life. Two years on, I sing with both SCC and the NHSingers, and find myself on my way to performing at Carnegie Hall! I also now run a choir at work, which is attended by both staff and patients, one of whom is now running it with me! I will always be grateful to have music back in my life, and using it to celebrate my mum.

Deborah Klayman

* * *

I have always loved music, playing, dancing or singing. When I was at school I was lucky enough to have free individual music lessons, played violin and sang in the choir. Music and singing was the most pleasurable escape. After leaving school it all stopped for a couple of decades. Then I started Ballroom and Latin dancing but had always wanted to get back to singing.

I joined Bournemouth Rock Choir in about 2011 about a year after Jenny started. I'd wanted to join for a few years. I was really keen to sing the kind of music that Rock Choir was offering but at the same time a bit hesitant to go alone the first time. When I took early retirement from my job in I.T. there was more time for hobbies, and it so happened that a friend of mine, a former colleague, had already joined Rock Choir and invited me to go along with her.

When I attended my first 'taster' session, I remember being struck by how Jenny just opened up to everyone about her journey with depression. I was stunned that someone could be so open and talk about her personal experience with these issues to an audience of strangers. Existing Rock Choir members were on hand to make us feel welcome with coffee and cake. I knew then that this was something really different. We were taught to sing 'Something Inside So Strong' that day and I resolved to join.

I was very nervous about performing but encouraged by Jenny's confidence in our abilities and sang in my first choir performance that first Christmas, four months after joining. We sang, it was a fabulous atmosphere and I loved the buzz of performing.

Jenny is an inspirational leader, and makes us feel valued. When you talk to her, she makes you feel that what you have to say matters, and listens, focusing her full attention on you. Her enthusiasm is infectious, endless and she is 'electric' with the energy she gives off.

Over the years it seems the better I know the material, the more confident I am in performances. I want to sing as well as I possibly can, and trust Jenny knows how to get the best from us. What works for me in performances, with the distraction of having an audience, is what she says. To watch her like a hawk, keep our eyes fixed on her all the time, and she will keep it all together.

Later in life whilst doing Open University (OU) courses, and also now with choir, there is a difficult to describe feeling of being part of a much bigger thing. It reminds me of when I was in the school orchestra, hearing my violin but also hearing the much bigger sound of the whole orchestra. In choir, the swell of the sound, all our different voices as they come together, singing our different harmony parts, is joyful. I haven't found many occasions that the word 'joyful' fits, but it truly fits singing in choir.

Another, rather unexpected, benefit came with some of the older songs we sing. For example, I wasn't looking forward to singing 'Clouds' by Joni Mitchell - which we learnt in Rock Choir - because I associated it with difficult teenage years. But as we learned the arrangement, took it apart section by section and put it back together, it became new, different and ours. When I hear it on the radio now – as with other such songs we have learned since - the memory is of how we sing it in choir and the sound we make, and the song has taken on a whole new meaning. Even the sad songs become uplifting. The emotional association with those songs from my youth has completely changed for me. A bit like rewriting history.

Some years ago I suffered from anxiety and a health condition that although not serious, made daily life stressful, with careful planning needed in order to leave the house. For some years I didn't know how to manage with it. The thought of getting on a train or bus, or go on a long journey was daunting and I would try to avoid this if at all possible. Being in places with a large number of people was also a big issue and I avoided events including my OU graduation ceremony.

These days I do all those things. Counselling was helpful but being in the choir has motivated me to 'go for it' and make changes, and that has built my confidence. Being in a hall with a lot of people is now something I don't worry about – we are all in it together. I also became hopeful that I could improve my health and after research and finding some help can now manage it effectively, which is very liberating. It almost feels too much to credit choir and singing with so much, but I think that performing in a choir can cause you think of yourself differently. OU made a big difference to my life in the past, and choir has made an even bigger difference now. I am now a person who takes part and performs, not a person who spends her time thinking about how to avoid crowds and travel.

When Jenny left Rock Choir, I knew I would miss her, but she is so multi-talented I felt it was inevitable that she would move on sometime. My thought was that at least I will be able to say that I sang with Jenny before she became a star!

Sweet Charity was then formed and she was back! I didn't join immediately as several family situations had developed which took up a lot of time and energy and Verwood was not very accessible. However, a year later, a Rock Choir friend, another Jan, encouraged me to join and I am so glad I have! Sweet Charity Choir is a great format and I find it complements Rock Choir and am a member of both. The two and a half hour session length allows more time for exploring the songs in depth which is very satisfying, and contributing to charitable causes and hearing the stories behind them, is an added bonus.

I love the fact that there are so many different personalities in the choir. We all fit right in. In the cake and coffee queue at rehearsals I have the opportunity to have interesting chats with people I haven't spoken to before. Everyone I have met has been kind, whether it is loyalty shown, a supportive hug or just saving a seat for someone who is running late, we all look out for each other. I have seen when choir members ask for help, others quickly volunteer.

I am really proud that the choir is going to sing in Carnegie Hall and that I am part of the choir, and although I won't be with them in New York I am look forward to taking part in other big events in the future.

When life is stressful Choir has been a sanctuary for me. I know that no matter how I feel when I go into a Sweet Charity Choir session, I will come out feeling 'balanced' and uplifted.

Jan Lewis

**Simply The Best**

I first met Jenny nine years ago at her first, and my first, Rock Choir rehearsal in Southampton.

She was such an inspiration to a non-singer (Oh Happy Days!)

So when she formed Sweet Charity I jumped at the chance of joining, because I just love the way she teaches, her comic timing, fun, laughter, funny faces, but most of all she makes me think that I can sing!

She brings out the best in us all.

Carol Harris

**See How It Goes**

Having brought up two young children alone, working full time and devoting everything to them I decided, as they hit their late teens, I wanted to do something for me.

So it was on 15 September 2010, I arrived (alone) at a church hall in Archers Road, Southampton – this was a new experience but I felt positive as I loved singing.

It had been a long day at work and a stressful drive to Southampton but I was excited, if a little apprehensive.

A very smiley, chatty young girl at a keyboard announced that this was a new venture to her really but we'd just 'see how it goes'.

The song we were presented with was an old favourite. I accidentally ended up at the 'lower end' of the group and we began work on: "Oh Happy Day".

Several years later I took a picture of that girl at her keyboard, thinking that was the last time I would see her, as she was moving on to other things. Little did I know that she would in fact take me with her to another choir, called Sweet Charity.

And here we are.

She continues to be inspirational. I became a permanent member of Sweet Charity and 'The Tea Ladies'. I have made lifelong friends who were so important when I later retired. I have helped raise thousands of pounds for copious charities; I have seen amazing courage from so many people and in front of me I have seen that young girl grow and grow.

Sometimes it has seemed just a flash since September 2010, other times it has seemed a lifetime of experiences and emotions – from 'Come Alive' to Carnegie Hall.

I am so grateful for every day I sing alongside friends I would never have met, looking at that same young girl who was just happy to 'see how it goes'.

Well, it certainly 'went' didn't it, Jenny Deacon?

Maxine Farmer
Retired English Teacher/Single Mum

**Making A Difference**

Up to my eyes in breastfeeding and nappies
No sleep, virtually no life.
Just a continual loop of trying to get through...
Singing made the difference!
It genuinely gave me my life back
Somewhere for me.
It would brighten my day and many days after.
Keep on singing!

Nerissa Wilkins

**Singing Is A Tonic**

My life has been very stressful at times. After losing my first husband at the age of 38 years, I found dancing helped me then – but you really must talk to people, as a lot of people find it difficult to talk to you first. As time went by life got easier when I remarried. My second husband is a lovely man, with two children. I didn't have any children of my own.

I was living in Hertfordshire at the time and was very happy. Then my husband went down with thrombosis and nearly lost his life, but got through that after some time.

Everything was going well and I was enjoying life again. But then my daughter-in-law was diagnosed with cancer and sadly died, leaving three children.

We moved to Dorset to be near that family. I started singing with Jenny Deacon at Rock Choir and then on to Sweet Charity.

The children are growing up now and our son has remarried. But then three years ago my husband was told he had throat cancer. He had a big operation, went through 6 weeks of radiation therapy and is doing quite well at the moment. A real fighter.

Singing with Jenny is a real tonic to me. I would always recommend it. What a joy Jenny gives to us all. We all love her dearly, I go home feeling elated!

Maureen Faulkner
Retired Care Worker


**Uplifting Choir**

I first heard about Sweet Charity Choir from a friend who had attended one of Jenny's workshops and had then decided to go for a taster session. I decided to go along myself, absolutely loved it and signed up that same evening.

Jenny's talent and enthusiasm is awe inspiring. She is a remarkable teacher with a wonderful vision that has become Sweet Charity Choir.

Having no musical background at all and being one of those people that always says, "Oh I can't sing at all," I am so happy to be part of this wonderful group. It really is open to all and when those harmonies come together, Jenny's magnificent arrangements have brought tears to my eyes on more than one occasion.

I can have had what feels like the worst day ever, but when I get to choir and start to sing, everything suddenly feels better and all of my worries and anxieties just melt away... it is truly uplifting.

Barbara Brady
Client Servicing and Support Consultant

**Why I Joined**

I joined the Choir because I love to sing, but am not particularly good except when singing with others.

The sound we get when singing together boosts confidence in an ability to produce music. It makes you feel good about what you have achieved together.

But a lot of that is down to Jenny!!
Sheelagh Wanstall

\* \* \*

We emigrated from South Africa in 1989, when my daughter was five and my son was two. My husband is British and because of the politics in South Africa at the time, we felt it was the best thing for us to do. We settled into life here and everything was going well until my son Shaun was about six or seven and he started having 'episodes' where he would shiver as if he was cold, which we thought was a bit odd, so we took him along to the doctor, who said it was just a nervous tic or attention-seeking and to just ignore it, which we did for a few months. By then other things had started happening and he would just blank out and stare for a few seconds. I would wave my hand in front of his face and get no response at all, it was like he wasn't there. This was happening every few weeks and we knew this wasn't right.

Then one day we were watching a television programme about epilepsy, which I knew nothing about at the time, apart from tonic-clonic seizures or grand-mal fits as they used to be known then. My husband thought this was what Shaun might have, but I dismissed it at that point. Shortly afterwards, I spoke to a nurse friend of mine who explained there are many different types of fits. To cut a long story short, we took him to the doctor and he was diagnosed with epilepsy and put on medication, which unfortunately didn't work. Over the years he has been on many combinations of anti-convulsants, until he was eventually diagnosed with Lennox-Gastaut syndrome, which presents itself in childhood. It is the most common type of intractable (difficult to treat) childhood epilepsy and occurs in between 1 and 5 in every 100 children with epilepsy. He was initially under Poole Hospital then transferred to Southampton Hospital and then to Great Ormond Street.

He remained in mainstream school until he was eleven receiving extra help and support, as the number of seizures he was having had increased and he was suffering injuries due to falling so much. He started wearing a protective helmet for his own safety as he had so many injuries to his face and head. When he was 12 he had a bad fall at Heathrow Airport when we were returning from a holiday and one of his front teeth was knocked out and he split his lip. This resulted in him having to undergo oral and maxillofacial surgery. What he went through was just horrendous and it has been very difficult for us all.

When he was eleven, he moved to Victoria School, but it wasn't quite the right place for him so I did a lot of research and got involved with the local epilepsy support group. It was then I found out about a place in Lingfield, Surrey, which at the time was called St Piers but is now known as the National Centre for Young People with Epilepsy. It is a school with a hospital on site where they can monitor the pupils and treat emergencies. We applied for him to go there and he initially had to undergo a six-week assessment. He stayed on the hospital block and we would visit at weekends. He was only eleven or twelve at this time. By the end of the six weeks they concluded that a placement at NCYPE would be beneficial. The local authority hadn't been able to identify a school locally that would suit his needs, so they agreed to fund him to go there. It was a heart-breaking decision to send him to NCYPE but we knew it was in Shaun's best interests. It proved the right decision because whilst there and being closely monitored, by adjusting his medication, they were able to reduce the number of daily seizure from between 6 - 9 drop seizures a day to between 5 – 7 a week. He continued having other types of seizures daily. He boarded at NCYPE until he was twenty-one.

Following on from the absences, he had started having complex partial seizures and tonic seizures where he would go stiff and then fall over whether he was sitting or standing, hence sustaining so many injuries. He would come back home every second weekend and for the school holidays. I actually did a charity sky dive for NCYPE and my husband and I walked up Ben Nevis for Epilepsy Action, which was amazing.

I was working through all of this at Bournemouth University but they were so accommodating and changed my contract to term time, so when Shaun was home I was able to be there for him.

Once he left the NCYPE, his social worker found a local care home in Parkstone, which is great. Shaun is also on the autistic spectrum, has behavioural problems and unfortunately learning difficulties as well. The amount of seizures he was having affected his learning development and basically his reading, writing, maths and comprehension stopped at the age of seven or eight. He's not able to focus for very long on everyday tasks and his understanding is limited. He does have verbal skills and loves football, watching television and enjoys playing Bingo with us when we visit. He especially loves dramas and romantic films. It's quite sad really because he has never had nor never will have a girlfriend, and he will say to us, "I'm not Shaun anymore," and will take on the character of someone in the film because he wants to be loved like them.

He cannot go out independently and has to be escorted by two members of staff wherever he goes. He is with four other young men ranging from eighteen to late thirties, all with their own problems and they all have twenty-four hour care. Shaun has two day-staff and one night-staff allocated to him.

His behaviour at the moment is a lot better than it has been over the last few years and I think that is because at my request there is now a psychologist involved. Not with Shaun, but with the staff to provide strategies to help them manage him and also to recognise (by looking at his body language) when he might be on the verge of being unhappy about something. He will sometimes have clusters of seizures and they do have to intervene with emergency medication to stop the seizures. This can happen up to five or six times a month. If, after 2 doses of emergency medication, the seizures don't stop, paramedics are called and he is taken to hospital to be monitored. I can compartmentalise my life quite well so that when I am at work, I'm at work and when I'm with Shaun, I'm with Shaun, but if I see the home is trying to phone me whilst at work my heart sinks because this usually means he is having or has had multiple seizures.

Whenever I start talking about Shaun or thinking about his condition and what he has had to go through I get upset. Shaun is thirty-one now and we have been through so much with him since he was seven. He had 6-7 years of 'normality' and then his whole future was taken from him. He lost his childhood and as it later turned out, any chance of a normal life. He is happy in his own world and doesn't realise what his life could have been, which is the only thing we are grateful for.

Of course, through all of this our daughter has also suffered. We were so taken up with dealing with Shaun's condition that we didn't realise what a tough time she was going through. She is three years older than Shaun, and was thirteen and going through puberty when the really difficult problems began with him, which is such a tricky time anyway. We had no idea it affected her so much. She is now thirty-five, married with her own child and lives in Israel. Every so often she will refer to something that happened years ago and how she never expected much as we, her parents, were so involved with Shaun.

I used to play a lot of sport in South Africa and played badminton and tennis when I first moved here but had problems with my knees and couldn't continue. My father enjoyed singing and used to play the piano. When we went on family holidays he would enter my sister, cousins and I in talent contests and teach us songs. A favourite was Edelweiss! Apart from that I had never sung before, although I also played piano as a child. I never ever thought in a million years that I would join a choir but seven years ago a friend of mine who was already in Rock Choir encouraged me to go, and I absolutely loved it. I loved singing, I loved Jenny, I loved the people and the whole atmosphere. I would forget about Shaun, forget that my husband had bowel cancer which, despite being caught early, needed surgery and there were complications which resulted in numerous stays in hospital over a period of 5 years. I could also forget my own health problems and just enjoy singing with others.

In August 2013 after a routine blood test, I was diagnosed with Essential Thrombocythemia, a form of blood cancer. Understandably, this came as a huge shock and knocked me for six. I underwent extensive tests and was put on a low dose of chemotherapy as well as two additional medications. It took over four years, countless visits to the wonderful Jigsaw Unit at Royal Bournemouth Hospital and six-weekly blood tests to stabilise my bloods. I will need to continue having my bloods checked regularly and remain on medication for the rest of my life.

I continued with choir for a while after Jenny left, until I left to join a bridge course - something I had always wanted to do. When Jenny formed Sweet Charity, a couple of friends who were already going encouraged me to go along saying I'd love it. I wasn't sure at first as it was being held on a Sunday and the weekends are when we see Shaun. I so wanted to go but couldn't see a way of doing it. My friend Sally told me about the Carnegie Hall performance and even then I thought there was no way I could learn all the songs, after all, the choir had been going for eighteen months. After further thought, I messaged Jenny to see what she thought and she said of course I could do it, so that was it, the decision was made to join.

The first practice I attended felt like coming home. I absolutely loved it. I didn't realise how much I had missed being part of a choir. It is certainly a place where I can forget all my troubles. Now of course I am trying to catch up with learning all the songs. I have the CD playing constantly in my car and listen to the songs whenever I can. They are all such lovely arrangements however I do find some quite challenging and struggle with remembering the words of some of the songs.

Singing in Sweet Charity Choir has given me something to focus on and for those few hours twice a month, all my problems disappear.

Beryl Grindrod#
IT Asset & Configuration Analyst

* * *

## A Musical Inheritance

I live in Rayleigh and work in Southend as a Wills and Probate Lawyer. I'm also Mum to a son and daughter, now in their twenties, and I'm an enthusiastic member of Sweet Charity Southend Choir.

I come from a musical family and have always loved music and singing. My grandfather was a conductor in a brass band, my Dad played the trombone and my two older brothers and I were coerced into playing brass instruments at a very young age – in my case the euphonium at the age of six, which was like a full-size tuba for such a small girl! My parents also signed me up for piano lessons with an elderly tutor who favoured classical music and for a number of years I took theory and practical exams at the London College of Music.

Teenage hormones then kicked in! I rebelled against the boring regime of endless scales and classical piano pieces. I wanted to be out having fun with my friends. I drove my family crazy playing my current favourite record non-stop and singing along until I had mastered it, at which point I'd move on to the next one. I bought

Smash Hits (pop lyrics) magazine every month and those hits of the late 70s and early 80s still come naturally. Little did I know this would be such good practice for Sweet Charity Choir many years later.

Adult life took over – I left school, got a job, bought a house, got married, had two kids, got divorced, trained as a lawyer (whilst juggling single parenthood and working) and married for the second time. In 2010 my lovely Mum was diagnosed with aggressive oesophageal cancer and I was her main carer until her death in 2011.

The sad loss of Mum caused me to reflect on the previous eighteen years and I realised that, since my first child was born, I had done nothing just for me as there had been no spare time for hobbies or pastimes. In early 2012 I decided to rekindle my love for singing and joined a local choir. This was before the advent of Sweet Charity, but the choir I found was great fun and lasting friendships were made through our shared love of singing. The barriers come down very quickly in a choir environment, even for shy or anxious people. I don't believe there is any other common interest quite like it – and it's such good fun!

Sadly, the local choir group closed after about five years, but then along came Jenny to form Southend Sweet Charity and we all migrated en masse. The little red-haired angel was sent to us and got us all singing together again. Hurrah!

So here I am, forty years on, once again learning lyrics and singing over and over to the harmonies, usually in my car now so no one else is subjected to it (although I do sometimes get strange looks from pedestrians and other drivers!)

Friendships made seven years ago still continue, and new ones are made. Life is so much better for being a member of this fantastic choir. Singing is a great stress-buster and after a tough day at work you can't beat it for "me time". It's almost impossible to let your mind wander to any other worries while singing. I just love it!

Gill
Lawyer

## It's The Atmosphere

To me, Sweet Charity Choir is quite simply an opportunity to soak up the unique atmosphere and sound created by the inimitable Jenny and her instantly recognisable red keyboard. Her love and enthusiasm for her craft shines through in all her arrangements from the more simple warm-ups right through to the long, challenging pieces. When she teaches a new song, the speed at which she brings it all together is quite unbelievable, and it is great to be a small part of it. It is of course a complete bonus that at times she is completely bonkers and is cat mad like me! Long may it continue. "Miaow and goodnight!"

Avril Bassinder
Company Secretary (Pensions)

\* \* \*

I have never been one of those people who has been bullied, friendless or particularly unhappy, but I think I have always wanted people's approval. I always felt that I had to 'be' something.

Since joining Rock Choir nine years ago and subsequently following Jenny on to Sweet Charity, I have experienced a total acceptance of just me with no expectations. It seems to have permeated the rest of my life too because it just doesn't bother me what people think of me anymore. I don't know if that is partly just me getting older, but I was in my mid-fifties when I originally joined Rock Choir, so wasn't exactly a youngster. I just feel much more relaxed about being me these days. When you come to choir, you don't have to explain yourself to anyone.

About seven years ago my sister, who used to live close by, moved up to Scotland, which was difficult for me, but the Rock Choir family just enveloped me and supported me through that time, which was so special. I have made some brilliant friends, we have been on holidays together, had weekends away together, and some of those good friends are also in Sweet Charity. I mix with people now whom I would never have come across before. We are such a wide range of ages with different circumstances and backgrounds but we all have a common interest.

It struck me when we were doing a warm-up exercise recently just what a fabulous sound we can all make together. I feel such joy, like something inside me just opens up and blossoms. I used to sing as a child with my Mum, aunt and sister and would even do solos which I wouldn't do now, I don't even do karaoke! There is still a little bit of me scared of hitting the wrong note.

As a youngster I was really into heavy rock music, so a rock chick really. Now I'm more like a crock chick! I just love music and frequently go to concerts, it is an important part of my life and I feel very sorry for people who don't feel that way or who can't 'hear' it in the same way. I couldn't be without music and it is just awesome to be a part of making such an amazing sound together.

After my childhood singing, I didn't sing again for years and years until joining Rock Choir. I just love it, and can sing out loudly with no worries at all. Even if you feel a bit fed up when you arrive, you feel so much better when you leave, and there is usually a lot of laughter involved. I feel like part of a bigger family. It is really difficult for me to put into words how it makes me feel, but it's food for the soul.

Jenny is a human embodiment of music and she gives so much of herself. She expects the best from people and she definitely gets the best from people. She is honest and gives part of herself to us as a choir and as a result, people go the extra mile for her. As a choir we are so tight and precise, which is all down to Jenny. No one wants to let her down. The experiences we have been offered through both choirs have just been amazing and I have had the added bonus of sharing it all with my husband, Colin. The combination of confidence and friendships gained from being a choir member have quite literally changed my life and I am so grateful and thankful for that.

Anne Fleming
Occupational Health Adviser

**Ferry 'Cross The Solent**

It all started for me when I saw a lady called Caroline on TV talking about expanding her choir and explaining that Rock Choir was for everyone, from any ability. When I went to Jenny's very first Bournemouth Lunch Rock Choir session back in 2010, I immediately realised that this was what I'd been looking for. It probably had a lot to do with Jenny herself of course – our little pocket rocket!

Through joining that choir – Jenny's choir – I found a joy I'd hoped was out there. I love singing. I love the way Jenny teaches, I love that she brings people together with a special mutual bond. I love the friendships that bond creates and the deep feeling of pride and well-being when we sing together.

It so happened that Jenny left Rock Choir at the same time as I moved to the Isle of Wight. I thought we would lose touch but then I heard she'd mooted the idea of starting a choir in Dorset that supported charities. I was so excited, especially as I knew I'd be back with old Rock Choir friends. But Verwood was just that bit too far to get to without a car, and the Island ferries are horrendously expensive.

I really enjoyed watching from afar as Sweet Charity went from strength to strength and was thrilled when Jenny let me know she was starting another choir in Southampton. It's not easy to get to as there are several modes of transport involved and I have to beg a lift back to the ferry terminal late at night, but it really is so worth it. I felt so happy when we started the first song; it made me quite emotional – Jenny D has that effect on people!

There are of course many good choirs on the Isle of Wight but nothing compares to Jenny's teaching. It's worth me travelling from the Island to enjoy the uniqueness of Sweet Charity.

Lesley Gee
Receptionist

\* \* \*

Like a lot of my generation I had an idealistic childhood growing up in the 60's. I trained as a dancer and was all set to go to the Royal Ballet. Unfortunately, I had an accident and hit my head which subsequently brought on my epilepsy which meant I was unable to continue dancing, at least not to that standard. I carried on for a while but it just wasn't the same and some years later I had a fit, fell down the stairs and sustained a fairly minor injury which wasn't treated properly and, to cut a long story short, I was confined to a wheelchair which put paid to any dancing. I just loved the performance element of dance and I really missed that a lot.

There followed many years of ill health and all through that time I was missing that something in my life. I vowed to myself that one day I would join a choir. Being a bit shy, I sat down with my friend to try and work out what choir we could attend and as I do Brownies and she does Guides, which night we could both do. We tracked down Rock Choir in Hedge End, which wasn't one of Jenny's, but it was local and we went along together. I absolutely loved it and it gave me that buzz, that something that had been missing for so long. I subsequently found out that singing creates endorphins in your brain which gives you that feel-good factor. My friend gave up not long after, but I continued on with it and quite honestly it has changed my life. I have ME now and it even helps with that. When I've been singing, good days follow as the endorphins give me an energy and a buzz. It also satisfies that performance element which I was missing and so love. I am certainly not a show-off and am quite shy, but you can perform behind a mask.

One day a friend of mine, Sally, who was in Rock Choir, was telling me all about Sweet Charity, which at that time was only in Dorset and I dismissed it as I don't drive and couldn't get there. Sometime later I saw on Facebook that Jenny was starting a choir in Hampshire, and it just happened to be a hundred yards from where I used to live. Although I had moved, it was still fairly local. That was it: I emailed Jenny and went along with no hesitation. It has been absolutely fantastic. I really thought nothing could top Rock Choir but this is something so different and Jenny herself is different. Everyone in the choir is important to her and it feels very personal. I get different things from both choirs, which is fantastic.

Since attending choir, my pain threshold has improved considerably and I haven't had to increase my morphine so much. I have to take a considerable amount but haven't had to increase it since joining choir. My ME is also better - it's not good, but it's better and generally my life has been enhanced. The health implications and improvements are very real. They say singing helps your health and I truly believe it does. Just before my mum died, she said that my attending choir had given her back her daughter that she had lost, given her back her Katie, which I thought was so sweet.

Mum was still alive when we found out about New York and she was adamant I was going as she knew how much I loved it, having been before. She so wanted to live long enough to see us come back and hear all about it, but it wasn't to be. I have been doing lots of fund-raising, and managed to raise five hundred pounds for our New York trip, selling my Christmas cards and sweet treats to choir members and hope to raise more money in the future. It has all come together for me now. I'm sixty this year, my health is improved and I get to have that once in a lifetime opportunity where I am doing something so incredibly special and, to top it all, performing in front of an audience, which I love!

Katie Yeates
Brownie Guider

* * *

I grew up in a show business environment, virtually raised in a dressing room as my parents were a hugely successful variety act in the fifties, appearing on radio and television both separately and as a well-known double act of the day. My mum was a singer and my dad a pianist and they appeared on some of the biggest television shows of the time including The Black and White Minstrel Show and The Arthur Haynes Show playing in some of the most prestigious theatres in the country, including an eighteen-month stint at the London Palladium with Arthur Haynes, Nicholas Parsons and Susan Maughan.

A lot of my early memories are of watching in awe from the wings of various theatres as the stars of the day performed their acts to laughter and applause. Memorable occasions such as standing behind Tania - the famous baby elephant of the time - as she waited to go on stage (yes, that really was allowed back then) and being treated to an elephant shower, soaking me from head to foot, which I guess served me right. Crying as I watched my mum doing a sketch with Morecambe and Wise because I thought they were being horrible to her, watching my mum sing Autumn Leaves with Tommy Cooper playing the piano and wondering why everyone was laughing as gradually leaves started falling from above and the wind machine swirled them around until you couldn't see either of them properly, but they carried on as if nothing had happened. Watching Ken Dodd in his heyday from the wings at the Opera House Blackpool as the packed audience were shrieking with laughter. I remember meeting Donald Peers with just his underpants on, Kathy Kirby giving me a big kiss on the cheek with her big red glossy lips, and Larry Grayson wearing a silk kimono, lying on a chaise longue in his dressing room dramatically feigning a headache. All these and many many more are dear and treasured memories. The world of entertainment has changed so much now and I feel privileged to have met these people. It was a wonderful era.

The flip side of being the only child of such talented and famous parents was that most people, including many family members, had this expectation of me to follow in their footsteps. Whenever anyone asked me what I wanted to be when I grew up, my reply was always, "I want to be a star". Whether this was because I really did or because it was what I knew they expected to hear I'm not sure, but the pressure and weight of expectation was enormous and led to deep feelings of inadequacy and not being good enough, which have lasted my entire life. I have always felt a huge disappointment to both sides of my family that I did not live up to my parents' high standards. Subsequently, this has created in me a firm belief that all children are unique in their own right and should not be viewed as an extension of their parents.

My happy little world came crashing down around me when I was eight years old and my dad, the centre of that world, whom I adored, died, cruelly taken from me aged forty-seven, and changing me and my life forever. As a little girl I used to spend many a happy hour singing along as my dad played the piano. There are a few songs to this day that I cannot listen to without crying as I am immediately transported back to that carefree time when I had my dad. Music has that incredible power to take you to any moment in your life, good or bad, and stir up emotive memories.

My mum is now in the advanced stages of Alzheimer's and in a care home for retired entertainers. Up until the last couple of years, music still resonated with her. It was the one thing that she recognised and that stirred her memory, particularly if she heard her own voice. I could see something light up inside her. Sadly, that is not the case now, but it is reassuring for us all as a family that her music lives on and the person she was will never be forgotten.

Being in a choir has helped me cope better with some of my deep-rooted beliefs. I have learned that it doesn't matter if I don't have my mum's amazing singing voice or my dad's brilliant song writing talent and extraordinary piano playing ability. What is important is that I am singing for enjoyment with nothing to prove, where no one is judging me, or my voice, as we are all in the same situation with our ups and downs, our quirky differences and surprising similarities. I am in two choirs, Rock Choir and Sweet Charity, both of which I absolutely love. I always laughingly tell people that I have a good choir voice and by that I mean I can sing out loud and proud in a group without fear, and contribute to the overall beautiful sound that many voices together can make. I cannot imagine life not being in a choir now. It provides me with a hobby, friends, a community spirit but most of all, for that little girl inside me, a true sense of belonging.

Kelly Reynolds

## So Shy

I had always been told I was tone deaf and couldn't sing. My Dad was a school teacher who used to teach our music class, and I was always being told to shut up as I was putting the others off. Consequently I would creep into the class trying not to be seen or heard. How ridiculous is that!

So all those years ago when I crept into Jenny's first class in Ferndown like a scared little mouse I didn't even know which section to join and changed my harmony choice at least five times. I had never sung before, not even in the house, and didn't have a clue where to sit.

Jenny came to my house and gave me a few private lessons. She told me that I was NOT tone deaf, as I had been brought up to believe.

Part of me is still that scared little mouse that doesn't want to be noticed, but our awesome Jenny has delivered us an amazing opportunity to go to New York and I will sing my heart out, and with every breath bless her.

Anon

## Sweet Charity To The Rescue

I have to admit I had a very good life. I was enjoying retirement with my husband Lee. The house was paid for, the children all settled in their own lives. We were free to enjoy a healthy, comfortable lifestyle with time to pursue our own interests.

After spending many years working for the NHS, Lee was now an enthusiastic member of the Volunteer force at Royal Bournemouth Hospital, spending a couple of days each week in a friendly familiar environment, leaving me free time to pursue my own interests.

I joined a Creative Writing group and found much pleasure in seeing my short stories in print (and I even managed to have a short novel published, which is still doing the rounds of local libraries!). I am an enthusiastic gardener and loved spending hours sorting out our small plot, and pottering in the greenhouse. But my true love was - and is – music.

I caught the singing bug when I was co-opted into the school choir and found fulfilment in becoming a part of the magic when voices blend. Church and community choirs followed for a few years but were abandoned when fulltime work and family duties became all-encompassing.

On retirement, missing my singing, in 2010 I found a new choir starting up nearby. I went along on the Monday evening, and found it was the very first session for all of us – including the choir leader, a charismatic, hugely talented and inspirational young woman by the name of Jenny Deacon. When I developed cataracts in both eyes and could no longer drive at night I switched to Jenny's daytime choir and found a whole new group of friends to bond with. We were all devastated when Jenny left to pursue her own ambitions, and the choir was never quite the same afterwards.

However, in February 2017 my cosy comfortable world came crashing down when Lee was diagnosed with bladder cancer - shockingly sudden with no prior warning and in a matter of days we were deep in the hospital system and I had to learn a whole new set of skills. I confess that I considered myself the world's worst nurse. Being a long-term Carer was my ultimate nightmare, and now here I was, responsible for a very sick 82-year-old man, and without a clue how to cope. With the invaluable help of the professionals we muddled along and between us we found ways to cope.

In May last year Lee had another problem to deal with when a blood clot was found on his lung – and I had to step up again and learn how to give his daily injections. But my social life vanished. My garden became my salvation, and I took out my frustration and my "it's not fair" moments in attacking weeds and taking the shears to shrubs and hedgerow.

Then I heard that Jenny was starting a new choir. Even better, it was in a location easily accessible for me. Sweet Charity Choir was initially to run for one year, with the object of raising £1000 for charity. Suddenly I was among like-minded people who quickly became caring friends, singing beautiful, challenging music under the direction of this amazing young lady, who somehow has the ability to teach anybody to sing anything! For a few hours each month I can get away from my worries, focussing on the words and notes on the page, frustration melting away. I have my life back! Sweet Charity is going from strength to strength, raising a great deal of money for a wide variety of charities. It seems to me that as Sweet Charity has grown, so Lee's health has improved at the same rate. He is now in remission and even managed to come to our Christmas concert – the first time he'd been to a social event in almost 2 years. Best of all, he is even getting back to Volunteering at the Hospital!

Bless you Jenny for Sweet Charity, and for being you!

Georgie Foord
Retired Personal Assistant, Writer, Novelist.

## Feel The Love – My Embarrassing Moment

I first started with the choir in 2017 but due to work commitments I didn't attend many, so missed out on the "Come Alive" recording. However, I started properly again in January 2018. I have no words only "Wow". Jenny is amazing with her musical talent and her personality and passion.

Every time I go to Sweet Charity rehearsals I feel so happy and, if you are on your own, Jenny will make sure you are not!

In June last year we did a big concert. The heat was horrible and this caused me to pass out on stage (blushes). I felt so embarrassed but the Sweet Charity family were amazing. I felt the love and the attention I got was mind blowing. Jenny even private messaged me to check I had got home ok and told me not to worry but look after myself. I will never forget the love and care of this day.

When I'm at Sweet Charity I forget all my troubles and woes as Jenny pushes you to get out the best sound. We chat, we have cake and we raise money for charity as well as enjoying ourselves.

I'm gutted to have missed a full month due to work, but oh, I'm sure looking forward to lots more Sweet Charity Choir in the future. I must also thank Den Carroll who initially invited me to Sweet Charity. Without joining I wouldn't have experienced so much and I'm so looking forward to New York in July. It will be amazing.

So one last note: Thank you Sweet Charity family and Jenny for (as she puts it) being part of my life.

Julie Hope
Shift Leader in a Dementia Care Home

**All About Friendship**

I have always been shy and struggle with low self-esteem and anxiety issues. The thought of standing on a stage singing in front of an audience was something I had never contemplated and yet here I am, doing exactly that.

Music has always been a huge part of my life. Some of my earliest memories involve listening to music with my Mum and being allowed to play records on her gramophone, her pride and joy. I never learned to read music or play an instrument but I have always loved to sing, even though I wasn't sure I was any good.

Friendships for me have often revolved around a shared love of music, favourite artists or genres and being part of a choir is about friendship and the love of music too.

I joined the choir for fun but it has become so much more than just fun. The pleasure and sense of achievement when we have learned Jenny's arrangements is immense. There is great camaraderie within the choir and the shared experience is joyful and uplifting.

Being part of Sweet Charity Choir has helped me to feel more confident and I am so proud to be a part of it.

Anon

## Good For The Soul

There is something indescribably emotional about singing with a group of people.

Whether this is during a concert with a bunch of complete strangers, singing along to a great band as they play your favourite songs, or at a football match perhaps, but especially when singing in harmony with a choir.

You may not even know the names of all the people around you, but you have an instantaneous bond; an unspoken, visceral response to working together to produce something (hopefully) beautiful.

It is instinctive to support each other as your voices rise and fall, interweave and move apart again. I think this is why it is so uplifting, and can lift your mood beyond reason.

Certainly as I was undergoing chemotherapy for breast cancer a few years ago I found that "going to choir" was one of my strongest anchors. No matter how nauseous or light headed I may have felt, within moments of being amongst those kind and caring singers, I forgot everything but striving for the best and enjoying myself.

I recall an outdoor performance just before Christmas one year. I was feeling pretty good, but I needed to wear a black woolly hat to keep my poor "baldy-heid" warm, so it was fairly obvious to those around me that I had little, if any, hair.

In self-consciously straightening my hat, I inadvertently flipped up half the collar of my fleece. The choir member behind me gave my shoulder a gentle squeeze and then straightened my collar. Thinking about this now makes me well up at that simple but kind and thoughtful gesture. We ladies all do that kind of thing don't we, but this felt special. It is THAT level of care and friendship that lifts mere acquaintance to a higher plane.

To be part of a choir truly is good for the soul. It reminds us that we are human; the same as our neighbours, and part of something huge. When we pull together, we can achieve so much.

And that moment of absolute silence, when the choir stops singing in perfect unison? Well it often takes my breath away.

Sally Grant
Small Business Owner/Operator

**My New Passion**

Although I've only been in the choir for a short time it's made me feel so good. I have talked about joining a choir for a while but it's never been the right time. I joined Sweet Charity in the summer and it was so great it has put me out of my comfort zone, and I can't remember the last time I performed in front of people (since my school years perhaps? … Let's just say a few years).

Our performance at Christmas was amazing. I was pretty nervous but once we all started singing I loved it. The next day I was buzzing and happy.

I'm so glad that I found Sweet Charity Choir. I think I have found another passion!

Claire Harrison
Curtain Maker

**Singing Is**

C companionship
H happiness
O opportunity
I inspiration
R reward

Jenny Park

**Practice Makes Perfect**

I first met Jenny at another choir, where she was the teacher. My neighbour took me along and I only intended to stay for one session. I'd been in church choirs as a child and hadn't enjoyed the experience so did not have very high expectations. But Jenny's enthusiasm and talent shone through and I was hooked.

When Jenny started Sweet Charity Choir I joined right from the start and have not looked back. My husband knows that choir sessions are sacrosanct and these dates in the diary cannot be changed!

For many years I've had ME and I find singing in a choir is a very uplifting experience. As well as the joy of singing, we have a lot of fun at the sessions too. There is great camaraderie at Sweet Charity. I have made lots of friends and enjoy sitting next to different people at our rehearsals.

Remembering all the lyrics and harmony parts is good for my brain (which tends to be on the sluggish side at the best of times).

I don't have the best voice in the world and I'm sure I'm an assault to Jenny's perfect pitch. She can pick out a wrong note at fifty paces but no one is ever singled out and although we may have to go over things many times until we get it right, it is always done with humour and love.

Having the opportunity to perform at Carnegie Hall is a chance of a lifetime (although a little scary) and I am looking forward to it. I know what I've got to do to get there – practice, practice, practice!

Not only do I get so much from the choir sessions, my husband and I have rekindled a shared love of music and now go to gigs – and even the odd music festival!

I get so much from the Sweet Charity Choir I feel Jenny should be made available on prescription, on the NHS!

Finally, to Jenny I would just like to say:
Thank you for the music, the songs we're singing
Thanks for all the joy you're bringing
Who can live without it, I ask in all honesty
Without a song (I can't dance) where would life be
So I say thank you for the music, for giving it to me.

Julie

**Stress-Buster**

I met Jenny when I joined New Forest Rock Choir right at its inception and I continue to love singing there. But when Jenny left, I so missed her musicality, sense of humour and friendship, and so I joined Sweet Charity Choir as soon as it formed. Sweet Charity Choir holds a really important place in my life: it's vital for stress relief, as well as being something that just makes me feel great!

A close family member has mental health problems, and for a decade I have been very much impacted by it. Some days I feel enormously stressed by their demands and difficulties, and the verbal abuse can be very hard to handle. Practising the choir songs makes me happy, and I look forward to rehearsals so much. Once I'm there, I focus totally on the music and that doesn't leave any room for the worry I have been experiencing. For three blissful hours I leave it all behind and live in the moment. Physically, I relax and breathe deeply, and emotionally I feel my spirits lift. And I always sleep so well that night!

Choir members are open and friendly and it's fantastic to share such a positive experience with like-minded people. I also feel the choir makes a difference as we collect for all kinds of charities. It's great to think that the wonderful cake is supporting good causes!

Sweet Charity rehearsals are the highlights of my month – I can't imagine life without this choir.

Anon

**A Chat With The Tea Ladies**

**Deb** - *I was the last of the four of us to join New Forest Rock Choir in January 2011, in Brockenhurst Village Hall. Kerrie and Rachel already knew each other, having joined in the previous September, but hadn't met Max (Maxine) at that point.*
*The normal question when you first join a choir is: "Where would you like to sit?" and my reaction was: "Oh, in the middle somewhere", which just so happened to be where Kerrie and Rachel were - in the alto section. They looked friendly enough so I asked if they minded me sitting next to them and of course they didn't, or at least that's what they said to me! By the end of the session we'd got each other's names and that was about it, but the following week I sat with them again.*

**Rachel** - *We were just saying the other day how we are like family and are so supportive of each other, and I also wouldn't have got through certain things without these guys. Kerrie and I met on the very first choir session Jenny held, literally as we were entering the building. Once we had established we were both going to choir we stuck like glue to each other from then on.*

**Kerrie** - *I remember that evening and wondering what on earth I was doing. I had just recently retired, having been a Headteacher and owning a private school. My favourite thing about school, and what I missed more than anything, was the children singing and me singing with them. Whether it was hymn practice, the school choir or collective worship, I just loved it. Whenever I could hear singing I would gravitate towards them and join in. So there I was, newly retired, and sitting on my own in a coffee shop in Lymington idly reading a newspaper that was lying around. In it was an article about Rock Choir, which said singing is for everyone, and no audition was required. I googled it when I got home and as luck would have it, Jenny was holding her first taster session a couple of weeks later, so I thought: "Why not give it a go?" I had never thought of myself singing, apart from with children, and that first night joining a choir with adults I was really questioning myself and felt such an impostor, which I still do to a certain extent. I've always been great at doing things in character, and performing or talking in front of the entire school was no problem, but with adults I have never really been secure.*

**Deb** - *When I first joined choir, I had just come out of hospital and I was feeling like I had lost myself within my marriage and my family. That wasn't a bad thing and I was quite happy being a mum and a wife but I had lost a little bit of myself along the way. I needed a hobby which was absolutely sacred to me. I knew I could sort of sing, so began looking for a choir and joined Rock Choir. It was on "cricket night" and I would sometimes find myself walking away from a match and missing my son's innings, which makes me sound like a really bad mother, but it was my two hours a week. It is so easy as a mum to say: "Oh, it doesn't matter, I will give it a miss this week," but I was absolutely adamant. This was my thing,* *nothing was planned around it or during it and it has actually got me through some difficult personal stuff, and of course it gave me the added bonus of meeting these lovely ladies.*

*I knew Brockenhurst Village Hall very well and I think it was during that first year I suggested to Jenny that we could make use of the kitchen facilities and raise money for charity at the same time by asking the choir to contribute to tea and coffee at rehearsals. Jenny thought it was a great idea so I roped Kerrie and Rachel in to help me. I can honestly say now that they have become my greatest friends. Choir has given me these ladies and I really don't know how I would get through life now without them.*

**Max** - *I had brought my kids up from the ages of three and one on my own. About ten years ago, when they hit their mid-teens, it just struck me: "What have I got that isn't work?". What really clinched it was when one of my daughter's friends called out to me in the street as "Katie Farmer's mum", which was fine, but I kept thinking about that. I suppose because there was just the three of us, I felt quite secure in that for a long time whilst they were small. I still feel that security of course but as they got older, I began to question what my future held. It was at that point that I came across a flyer in one of the coffee shops in town during that summer break and decided I would just turn up on my own to Archers Road in Southampton. I'm not a nervous person but I was quite nervous going to that first rehearsal. What made it better was that Jenny was brand new too and probably equally nervous.*

**Rachel** - *I am a teacher and at the point I joined choir, I had been going through a bit of a hard time, in as much as I had lost my voice for six months and was literally barely managing to whisper, following laryngitis combined with speaking too much. I had to re-train my voice to talk, but my vocal chords hadn't returned to normal, despite going to speech therapy twice a week for about four months. About a year previously, I'd seen Rock Choir on the television and thought how I'd love to be involved in something like that, but at the time there was nothing in the vicinity. When I was approaching the end of my speech therapy around June or July, my speech therapist told me how singing would really help me to get* *my voice back, so I looked again and, lo and behold, there was a taster session nearby for Rock Choir. I felt it was meant to be. Nobody else I knew at the time wanted to go and I'm not usually very good at trying things on my own, preferring to be in a group but I decided to give it a go as I had nothing to lose. When I first met Kerrie walking in, I was still barely managing to whisper.*

**Kerrie** - *I could hardly hear what she was saying at that taster session. She was much better by the time we started properly in the September, although not fully. I remember it took a while for her voice to develop.*

**Rachel** - *It really did, I was without a voice for about six months in total and I remember thinking seriously about my career as it was based around my voice. I truly thought I was going to have to look for something else. Having not been at work for all of that time, I felt quite down as well so before going into choir that very first time I was sitting in my car in the car park for quite a while doubting myself and wondering if I could do this. In the end I gave myself a good talking to and plucked up the courage to go in, which is when I met Kerrie...*

**Kerrie** - *And all the while there was I, wondering what I was doing there!*

**Deb** - *It's like a force field had spun us all together.*

**Max** - *It really is. I think Jenny was going through a similar thing as she told me she couldn't get out of her car either. I just turned up for the very first session Jenny ever did at Archers Road in Southampton and Jenny suggested I attend the Brockenhurst choir as I lived in Hythe, so although it was a longer journey it would be easier. I remember sitting in front of the others and this fly was buzzing around us. In one swift karate style move I killed it dead and that was it, we got chatting. I think I impressed them so much.*

**Deb** - *She was a ninja ...*

**Kerrie** - *Yes we thought we could do with someone like her!*

**Deb** - *Max has always got a story, and is the great raconteur of the group. Once she retired from teaching, we recruited her into the tea ladies, which has now escalated into us regularly going out to various locations to drink tea, eat cake, maybe celebrate each other's* *birthdays but more often just to chat and put the world to rights.*

**Max** - *We would never have met under any other circumstances, as we live quite far apart.*

**Kerrie** - *And we are completely different ages, but it makes no difference and that in itself is so wonderful.*

**Deb** - *We get really thrown these days if we can't perform in our correct line or at least in two twos....*

**Max** - *And if we get on the wrong side of each other that's it, we can't do it ......*

**Rachel** - *When we are lining up for a concert we are all desperately trying to be together ...*

**Deb** - *We literally cannot function unless we are a single unit!*

**Kerrie** – *And of course Jenny is ultra-special to us. There aren't any words really to describe her. Her influence on all of us has been absolutely tremendous.*

**Max** - *I really thought that when I took a photograph of her last Rock Choir session, that would be the last time I would ever see her. Everyone was heartbroken and we couldn't sing. I sometimes wonder what would have happened if I had stayed in the Southampton choir. I certainly wouldn't have met or been part of the tea ladies.*

**Kerrie** - *We have watched Jenny grow and seen the effect all of this has had on her, which in turn makes us so happy.*

**Deb** - *We are also incredibly protective of her. Don't anyone dare say anything negative to or about her or you'll have to face us! She's got a mum but she has hundreds of aunties too! The thing with Jenny is she is honestly and truthfully a kind, loving, positive person who worries about other people and that reflects back to her. She has been openly vulnerable and we have got particularly close to her in the past on a personal level as we used to hang around after choir and help her put the chairs away. Of course we followed her to Sweet Charity and there was no question, teas were always going to be part of it because it had proved such a success in Rock Choir. It's a time to socialise and get to know the whole choir family not just those sat next to you and for Jenny it's always about family. Plus of course cake is always a winner! I think* *because of her willingness to share, it helps other people to feel very secure. Jenny's choirs are safe places. You can come along with anything, a mental health issue, a physical vulnerability, or a passing problem in your life. Everyone is accepted for who they are. I have cried in choir because it's brought up stuff, but I don't feel embarrassed because I know I am completely supported. There are very few places or clubs you can join which are that safe.*

**Rachel** - *Jenny is so giving and has been so helpful. When I had to have half my thyroid removed and lost my voice again, I didn't think I was going to be able to sing. She told me to just come along and do the warm up then to go. She gave me some exercises to do, which was brilliant because again I had lost my confidence. Twice now Jenny has helped me get my voice back, to literally find my voice, for which I will never be able to repay her.*

**Kerrie** - *It's incredible the way things have developed for all of us and the journey we have all been on. I would never in a million years have dreamt of being part of a choir like Sweet Charity. She gets the best out of every single person. I'm a bit of a perfectionist and cannot stand mediocrity and with Jenny you give the best you can, whatever your best is, and you always try that bit harder. I love the nit-picking. That's what it's about for me.*

**Deb** - *Jenny conducts with every bit of her face and body. She gives face and expects that face back which helps with the performance. The little hints and tips she gives to make the different sounds makes all the difference to the end result.*

**Kerrie** - *When we found out about the New York opportunity I was away on holiday and I honestly thought the others were having me on at first. I think I was half way up a Greek mountain with no internet and when we got to the nearest place where I could check my messages, and particularly my Tea Ladies WhatsApp group, I had missed hundreds of messages! As I scrolled through I saw the one which read, "Kerrie, guess what! We are going to perform in Carnegie Hall, New York!" It took a while to sink in! It's so exciting and we feel very lucky indeed!*

\* \* \*

I was diagnosed with breast cancer two years ago, just as Jenny was starting up Sweet Charity. Being in the choir has really helped get me through. I have always enjoyed singing and attended a convent school where I was in a madrigal choir and we even recorded an LP in 1979, which was lovely.

When I'm singing at choir, rehearsing at home or out walking with my dog, it means I'm not thinking about if my cancer is coming back, which is a relief as I constantly have that nagging voice in my ear saying: "is it coming back, is it coming back?" and that is really hard, so singing and rehearsing is an absolute release for me.

I am still undergoing treatment, and go to hospital for an infusion every six months, so it is still a big part of my life but I have now returned to work, albeit on reduced hours (30hrs a week) as I just get too tired. But the way I see it is, I'm alive and that's okay! I've always been a really positive person, but the one thing going through this has left me with is I now worry more than I have ever worried before. It hasn't given me that 'isn't life wonderful!' attitude. Instead I am always questioning: "What if? Shall we do this now because there may not be a tomorrow? I may not be well enough tomorrow. Will I still be able to do this the same time next year?" I have always been a very active person and enjoy paddle boarding Pilates and dog-walking. My partner and I have a VW T5 camper van, which we are always out and about in.

I didn't 'find' my cancer. In fact, I went along for a smear test and I happened to have a little mark on my breast which I asked them to look at. As a result, they put me on antibiotics for a week. When it didn't go away, they sent me for an ultrasound, which revealed it to be an ulcer. However, it also revealed a tumour at the back of my breast. I feel like somebody must have been looking after me, because I have since been told that if it wasn't for that ultrasound, it might not have been found, as it was so far back I would never have felt it. I always urge anyone to please check yourselves regularly and if there is anything at all different in your breasts just go and get it checked out.

I was in Jenny's Rock Choir previously, joining in 2011 and still attend to this day. However, I was gutted when she said she was leaving. I remember there was a palpable intake of breath from the whole choir when she told us she was going. When I first started with Sweet Charity I was having quite a lot of treatment, lost all my hair and as a result lost all my confidence, so told Jenny that much as I would love to be a part of it, I couldn't guarantee that I would make it to every session. It was a long way to travel from Southampton and I just didn't know what the future held. But I am here to say I have made it through and I'm proud of that.

I kept the same hairstyle for years, so losing my hair was a really big deal as it would be for most women. It is our crowning glory and I never thought I would change my style. I had a couple of wigs, one pink and one purple but found them too uncomfortable to wear. I got together with a henna artist and experimented with various designs on my head, which I loved. Instead of seeing cancer when I looked in the mirror I saw art and it was beautiful. I would encourage anyone who loses hair to cancer or alopecia to consider it as they may enjoy a henna crown.

After I was diagnosed, I went to see both my sisters and urged them to get checked, which they did and my older sister, to whom I am very close, also had a tumour. I like to remind her every so often that I saved her life, but joking apart I probably did. She is okay now and didn't require chemotherapy so has recovered very well. I found that coping with her being ill was much harder than dealing with my own illness. I think we are all a bit like that, you don't really worry about yourself and just get on with it, but when my sister was diagnosed, I suddenly knew what it was like to worry about someone else. Although we went through it together, we coped in very different ways. My sister worries about absolutely everything and I am the complete opposite.

Music is a big part of my life and I have a massive music collection. I cannot be in a room without having music on. I have a dog and walk for two hours every day with my headphones on. We did a song by Keane in choir last year 'Somewhere Only We Know'. At the time, my previous collie had also been diagnosed with cancer and I knew she wasn't going to make it, so that song and its lyrics really reverberated with me.

Going to New York with the choir is a big thing for me. I have only ever been on a plane for four hours before and have never done a long-haul flight. My other half has always tried getting me to go to Barbados or suchlike, but I don't like flying and I don't like heights. If I can get to New York without too many issues then I hope to be able to go on a long-haul holiday next year. I will put my music on and not look out of the window. Mind you, the last time I put music on to distract me on a plane, I failed to notice my other half was not feeling very well and he passed out!

I have made so many friends in choir, people whom I would never have met in any other way, although I have since found out one of my choir friends lives in the same area as me. Needless to say we car share now! I find it a very cohesive experience. Singing takes me on another journey where you just can't think of anything else. My mantra is 'singing is healing' and one day I will probably get a tattoo of that.

Laura Hewett
Help Desk Assistant, Southern Health NHS

**Charity Begins…**

When I first sang with Jenny, I did it to 'try it out'. Little did I know it would change my focus and give me so many other benefits. I now can't imagine life without getting my choir fix with Jenny. It's so uplifting and therefore surely has to have multiple health benefits both mental and physical. To feel so good after an afternoon of intense learning is amazing and I sleep like a log!

Physically it certainly helps with my breathing and asthma control simply by making me more aware of when to breathe!

Before Sweet Charity my charitable donations were a bit of a scattergun approach but I have enjoyed being educated about charities which I wasn't aware of previously. I now have a particular interest in small local charities.

Tricia Edwards
Retired Civil Servant

* * *

My mum and I joined Sweet Charity after seeing my friend perform with the choir in the summer concert. She'd kept saying I should join and my reply was always that I couldn't sing, but she insisted that it didn't matter and explained how it all comes together and sounds really lovely, so Mum and I eventually decided to give it a go.

Our first experience was the Greatest Showman workshop, which was a day long workshop learning a medley, which was probably one of the hardest but we loved it. It was a bit daunting as we didn't know anyone apart from my friend Chris, but we came in and sat down in the bass section and Chris came over to explain the different sections and that we might eventually want to move to altos. I did in fact end up in lower altos. Everyone was so friendly that first day and said hello and we chatted to various people who made us feel really welcome. I'm not very good at meeting new people or even talking to people so it was really great that the other choir members were so friendly and put us at ease.

I enjoy coming along so much and really look forward to the sessions. We are even going to New York with the choir which I can't quite believe. At first, we weren't going to, but after doing the Christmas concert, we got such a buzz from it that we felt we had to sign up for more. I was so nervous at that first concert and when I walked on the stage, I was convinced I wouldn't remember all the lyrics, as there are so many to remember. It's strange, but as soon as you start singing, the words just come out! As long as you keep your eyes on Jenny, everything is fine! She's amazing and so talented, I don't think people realise just how much effort she puts in. I can read music and used to play the flute and guitar. I haven't played much recently but feel I have reconnected to music now and maybe I will pick it up again in the future. I never thought I could sing, but the way Jenny teaches, you just get it and I find I can pick it up really quickly.

I also feel so much more confident now in terms of just talking to people. Going to New York is way out of my comfort zone, plus I don't do flying very well so it will be a bit of a challenge. I also don't cope very well with being out of control and I like to have everything planned so that will be difficult for me. I'm sure it will be fine though as we are all in the same boat.

I've always been a worrier, but in recent years have suffered regularly from anxiety and panic attacks. They usually start with a negative or dark thought and quickly spiral downward, where I start thinking of someone dying. It's really horrible, I start sweating, my heart races and I can't sit still. They usually, but not always, occur at night time and I have lots of stuff going around my head - all the 'what ifs' from the previous day - and I find that music really helps lift me out of that state. As a result, I am always listening to music and even use it for meditation. It's quite therapeutic and an important tool in my life. I am on a little bit of medication but generally try and manage it as best I can through other means and different therapies such as Reiki. I want to come away from medication and singing is part of that process. I'm guilty of scrolling through social media, especially at night time, which I am convinced doesn't help. Everyone seems to be on holiday or having a great life apart from you. Of course it's not true and they're not going to put the bad bits, but it still affects me.

Back in November, I had quite a bad spell of attacks so I did have to miss one choir session. I was in a really dark place and I wasn't able to do anything or even go to work. I couldn't be on my own, so had to stay with Mum for a bit. However, the first thing I did after this period of panic attacks was to come to choir. I only managed half of that session but even so, everyone was really lovely, and just to be able to come and sing for an hour or so definitely helped me out of that zone and the feeling that I was trapped. I am back on track now and feel that choir gives me something to aim for and something to look forward to, especially with New York coming up, and on the occasions when I have nothing to do or feel a bit bored, I get the music out and sing along. I have it on in the car and play it everywhere I go. Chris and I often put the full choir on at work and she sings her bass whilst I sing my lower alto and we put each other off!! It's great fun though. I really believe music connects everyone.

Lizzie Harrison
Finance Manager/Bookkeeper

## Something Borrowed, Something Blue

"Wear something blue," she said. "Any shade of blue. So we'll all look good for the recording."

I was pleased, Blue is "my" colour – but not always that easy to find.

Thinking about it, it's going to be November, and the hall is not that warm. Obviously a short sleeved blouse or t-shirt will not do. I've got a pretty jumper in sort of royal blue. Maybe I can wear that.

"No jeans," she said. "Navy blue trousers or skirt." The only skirt I've got is denim so that's no good. Hopefully my navy cotton canvas summer trousers will be OK.

So we all duly rolled up for our "Big Sing", with our blue outfits in bags and on hangers. I wore my navy trousers and jumper, with a big check shirt over the top. It was a good idea – when time came for us to smarten up for the video I just had to whip off the shirt!

All around me people were struggling into their shirts, blouses and dresses – wow, what a variety of colours and patterns! All shades of blue from sky to darkest navy and everything in between, and stripes, spots and frills and flounces.

The recording went well, *very very* well. What it led to was a big surprise to us all.

The next time we wore our blues, it was mid-summer and one of the hottest days of the year. This time I had some smart tailored trousers and a pretty light blue lacy blouse. However it became clear from the photos and videos after the concert that we all needed to be more colour-coordinated. So navy blue top to toe became the rule.

For the Christmas concert I stuck with my trousers and bought a smart navy blue blouse. I thought I looked fine; however all around me more and more ladies were gravitating into lovely dresses. I haven't been a "dressy" sort of gal for years so felt slightly under-dressed, like the party guest who misinterprets "smart casual".

So, as a result of that recording back in November, we're off to New York in July. I'm determined to do better and not let myself down.

I do a lot of shopping from catalogues and online so went into over-drive.

From my catalogue I ordered a knee-length wrap dress with three-quarter sleeves. That didn't quite do it for me. My boobs didn't do justice to the wrap top and it was too snug over my tummy. I don't have a lot of spare flesh but it manifests itself in all the wrong places. The dress went back.

Then I found a midi-length dress with short sleeves. Hmm. My arms at my age don't do a lot for short sleeves. But the dress was fine, and I could find a fine-knit shrug to go over the top.

Then I realised I would have to wear tights. The thought of struggling into a pair of new tights in what might be a cramped changing room in the company of around 100 other ladies also struggling into their tights was appalling! So what to do? I would have to go "long" so I could wear pop socks. I searched the web sites for a suitable garment. Amazon was hopeful, but nothing really jumped out at me. My catalogues all had their summer ranges in light, bright colours.

Then I found The Dress. In the back of my wardrobe, a forgotten survivor from the last cruise my husband and I enjoyed before his illness took him over. Long, floaty, with velvet bodice and cap sleeves and undeniably, truly, Navy Blue!

Georgie Foord

## What Singing And Music Means To Me.

"My soul connects with all the choir's souls through music. In joining Sweet Charity I have connected with some beautiful souls."
Kim Hamilton

"Sheer joyfulness."
Margaret Kimmens

"Singing is healing."
Laura Hewett

"Music has always been a huge part of my life. As a teen in the 60s I was enthralled by all the amazing music & pop bands, particularly the Beatles. My love of music has never diminished."
Linda Lee

"One of my proudest moments was singing in a choir in the Royal Albert Hall when I was 17. At last I have the pleasure of singing in a choir again nearly 50 years later."
Pauline Henry

"Brings me such happiness and healing."
Clare Bailey

"A release of emotions."
K.D

"Togetherness and Happiness."
Tina Loughlin

"Escape from everyday to somewhere wonderful."
Georgie Foord

"Being a part of something great."
Margaret Kimmens

"Music makes my soul sing."
Kim Hamilton

"Makes you feel good."
Anon

"Singing in the choir is a wonderful experience – full of joy and a great way to share with others."
Linda Lee

"Food for the soul."
Anon

"Totally committed 'in the moment' and forgetting everything else."
Pauline Henry

"Escapism."
Tina Loughlin

"Music is in my blood."
Kelly Reynolds

"I've a history of mental illness since my teens. This is the first time I've stuck to anything- it stops me from being a recluse."
Anon

"Makes me so happy and I love being part of the family."
Maureen Martin

From members of the Alto section

# Show Your Appreciation For
# The Serenading Sopranos

Layers like an Onion

The day started and was a bit of a funny 'un
So chilly, we all felt like a cold pickled onion
A white precipitation sent to ruin our plans
For all the eager Sweet Charity Choir fans
But the coach forged on full of excited chums
Full to bursting, seats under bums
It's nice to have a warm up, prepares for singing, we find
Freedom, The Chain, and Empire State of Mind
As a promo for our trip to Carnegie Hall
New York, New York, we're gonna have a ball
A recording on the coach, Nikki volunteers
She's our techno wizard, or so it appears
We sing our hearts out 'big lights will inspire'
Sweet Charity Choir - baby you're on fire
Sadly, record wasn't pressed during our rendition
We'll have to do it all again, that is my suspicion
Arrival in London, what we gonna do?
A mass of navy women, dash to the loo
Most important task, we've all pee'd
Bonding in the 'lavs' thats what we need
'Guess how many layers I got on today'
'A vest, a t-shirt, and thermal tights' they all say
A jumper, thermal socks, and a layer of lanolin grease

Salopettes, big undies and a really warm fleece
This is what's needed when Busking at the South Bank
Over-dressed in padded jackets and the size of a tank
Hoping the temperature will raise so we can peel some layers
Our little frozen hands and feet, someone hear our prayers
Stopping now and again for hot mulled ciders
Hoping this will thaw once it's inside us
As well as singing and eating, and social caring
All in navy blue, the whole 'family' are wearing
Like sisters from another mister, and Owen, Mark and Nick
We marched back and forth, pretty darn quick
Recording and video, camera stills
To catch our moments, our vibratos and our trills
And there's our Jenny pulling the best out of us
Before its time to get back on the snowy bus
But the snow has gone, the singing stops, now its time to go
And rest the vocal chords until the next show

Jilly Firmin

* * *

I joined Rock Choir on the very first session that Jenny ran in Bournemouth at Glenmoor School. My friend told me about it and asked me to go along with her. I agreed as I thought it would be something nice to do together. I had sung before with my performing arts school so I knew I would enjoy it. I certainly didn't think of it in terms of it being beneficial or therapeutic in any way, which it turned out to be.

My Dad died in 2004 and my marriage ended 4 years later. We didn't have children together. Outwardly I seemed to cope, but I suppose I was a little bit lost after that. Don't get me wrong, I was making the most of my new-found freedom and going out a lot with friends, but something was missing. I got to my mid-thirties and, after some serious thinking about what I wanted to do with my life,

I decided I didn't want being single to stop me having children. I looked into IVF but decided it wasn't for me. I had already been to a couple of meetings about fostering and discovered that on average there were about 90 children in the borough of Poole at any one time who didn't have homes. To me it felt selfish to go and create another life, not really knowing what the future held for me or how I'd be able to finance a child. Subsequently I went down the route of fostering.

Fostering is a very difficult process and you have to leave your dignity at the door. They delve into every single aspect of your life. At one point, I put the whole process on hold for about two months as they wanted to contact my ex-husband for a reference. The rules were they have to approach every single person you've ever lived with for a reference whether you had children together or not. I did not want that contact opened again. I didn't even have any contact details for him. Eventually, I decided this wasn't going to stop me proceeding, so I reluctantly agreed for them to contact him through his work address. Luckily, although they traced him, they didn't get a response. Apparently, once they've made contact, if they don't receive a response after a certain amount of time, they write it off and move onto the next stage of the process.

There were many more hurdles. For example, one of my very good friends at the time wrote a glowing reference for me which was checked and verified. However, sometime afterwards, she stopped contacting me and I later found out she had retracted her reference and told some untruths. I still don't know the reason for this and it was all very strange and upsetting at the time. Needless to say I haven't had any contact with her since. You certainly find out who your friends are through the process.

My son Harrison was the first child I ever fostered when he was eight years old. I started providing his respite care once a month initially for six months, during which his circumstances changed through the courts and he needed a long-term placement. At that point he was with a short-term foster family, so I offered to take him on a long-term placement. He was just nine years old and by then I'd fallen in love with him. I decided there and then that I couldn't let anybody else have him. It was an easy transition.

We continued to have a lot of trouble with Harrison's birth mother and Social Services asked if I would consider adopting him. Of course I said yes and if I'd known earlier that I could have adopted him, I would have done that from the start. The battle began to protect my son and it certainly was a battle. There was just me on my own competing against a traditional '2.4' family. I went through a very testing court case, which lasted about eighteen months and caused me a huge amount of stress, but thankfully I did eventually win a simple closed adoption, meaning no further contact with birth family until he is 18. I gave up my extremely successful and lucrative career, which enabled me to travel the world in style and live the high life, to take a much lower paid job earning less than I did when I was in my early twenties. It was no sacrifice to become a mum to Harrison.

Sadly, the difficult adoption process and previous events in life took its toll without me realising and I started suffering with anxiety. This really surprised me as I had always perceived myself as a strong person and wasn't really tolerant of anyone with a mental illness, believing they should just 'pull themselves together'. I didn't believe in it and then suddenly it happened to me.

It started at work. I went from being a confident person to getting embarrassed, afraid to speak up in meetings, groups or even on a one to one basis. I think I hid it well, which most anxiety sufferers do. We find coping mechanisms - breathing techniques, safety regimes. I was quieter than normal but I was like a duck - apparently calm on the surface but underneath the water, I was paddling hard to stay afloat. On very bad days I experienced shaking, stuttering, not being able to think straight, sweating, clammy hands, paralysis in meetings, paranoia etc. We over analyse the situation before we go into it. I became afraid of everything including driving (which was my livelihood) and even meeting friends. On better days, I had all of these symptoms but was able to control them just a little bit better. Even up to six months ago at Sweet Charity Choir, I would still walk in and need to sit near the door in case I needed to make a quick escape! I would feel anxious for the first hour until I got into it. However, I forced myself to get on with life and continue with situations that I was no longer comfortable with, which was extremely hard. I did have to remove myself from stressful situations a couple of times rather embarrassingly. I never had a full-blown panic attack but came extremely close to it. I shall never forget those moments but I'm here now, stronger than ever. I did find that when I eventually started telling others about it, a lot of people could relate to anxiety. Perhaps they had experienced similar symptoms themselves or knew someone that had. A couple of people I told appeared to have even worse symptoms than I did, which was strangely reassuring. My thinking started to change when I realised I was not in a minority. Plus I was a mum and I had to get on with it and show Harrison I was normal and strong. I will always have that unwelcome friend sitting on my shoulder and not a day goes by when it doesn't visit me in some small way but now it's under control.

I received lots of praise from a variety of people and not just those close to me about how what I had done for Harrison was amazing and how well I'd coped with the gruelling process. This all helped to boost me up again eventually. My friends and family supported me but, as anxiety is such a difficult thing to explain to people, I probably shut them out a lot of the time and pretended everything was fine. I didn't think they would be able to relate to anxiety or understand it.

After several visits to the doctor and various therapies including hypnotherapy and CBT, none of which worked, I managed to get it under control. My doctor convinced me that if I had a headache, I would take a tablet, so why suffer any longer? So, I agreed to mild medical intervention, which has really helped.

Rock Choir also helped considerably at the time and now of course Sweet Charity Choir. As well as the feel-good factor of our rehearsals, we have so many fantastic opportunities, We once sang at the Olympic Torch handover ceremony in Southampton for the London 2012 Olympic games, which I will never forget. I loved the vibe of our Christmas concert at the Verwood Hub 2018.

Of course, I have Harrison now and 2 loving cats – Max and Millie, who bring me great happiness and make everything worthwhile. We are a family. Of course at times it is really difficult being a single mum but it's what I expected it to be and I was totally ready to become a mum when I started down the fostering route. I'm happy not going out very much and just hanging out with Harrison (when it suits him). He's fourteen now and a typical teenager, a total Kevin! Having been through so much in his early years, he has turned his life around with support and guidance from me. He doesn't have any major lasting effects from his childhood at the moment and I am proud of the person he is becoming. I am also proud of myself for giving him this opportunity to live a happy and fulfilled life full of happiness. I have no regrets about my life and would do it all again in a heartbeat.

Harrison has a half-brother, who over the years has become like another son to me. He has a partner and a baby so I'm now a Grandma even though I am far too young obviously! Gradually we have become an extended unconventional family which is lovely. We do lots of special things together – days out, hang outs. I look after my Grandson overnight every so often to give them a break, which I love. I've not only gained a son but an entire family. It was totally my choice to maintain that contact, on my terms, and Harrison's brother often thanks me for that. I don't think he expected to see his brother again once the adoption had gone through. You have to do what's best for your child and the boys had always had a close relationship so I wouldn't want to stop that without good reason.

When Jenny left Rock Choir, I couldn't get my head round it. She was such a special, unique person. I remember once when we had a Rock Choir Christmas party and I think we were all doing karaoke. Jenny stood up and sang "I'll be your clown". I will never forget that moment - everyone was transfixed on her and her voice was absolutely amazing. She is so professional and brings our performances to such a high standard. I found out about Sweet Charity sometime after it had started and so missed the first eight or nine months. Once I realised it was Jenny, I joined immediately and have never looked back. I think if it was anyone else it wouldn't be the same. Harrison has been to all our concerts and even comes along with me to rehearsals when I have childcare issues. He sits at the back with his headphones on and his IPad and moans a bit about how bored he is. Jenny has been fantastic about it. I know he secretly listens as he makes comments about us sounding really good afterwards. He is our biggest fan and has a secret crush on Jenny (sorry Harrison! And Jenny!) He loves music and actually has a good singing voice but unfortunately he lacks the confidence to do anything with it outside of home. It's not cool at this age!

Life is good now. Between medical intervention and choir, I have my anxiety under control. It controlled me for seven or eight years but not anymore. I have noticed I have got more confident at choir in the last six months or so because of this, and no longer want to be hidden at the back! Jenny and our Sweet Charity Choir family are a very important part of my life and my family's life. My 'groupies' come to as many performances as possible. I'm proud to be part of such a powerful organisation, which raises money for charities and gives each member of the choir special memories. Jenny's talent and personality is infectious and unique and I thank her from the bottom of my heart for doing what she does - making us sing to the best of our ability, creating inclusivity for all and making us laugh a lot! I'm looking forward to being part of an exciting future for our choir.

I can't wait for New York. What an opportunity to sing at Carnegie Hall and visit the city for the first time. I will be supported in the big apple by some close friends and of course Harrison. He is so excited about going and his friends are really jealous!

Sarah Franklin
Sales Manager

**Singing In Southend**

My name is Jane Taylor. I live in Leigh-on-Sea and have been part of the Southend Sweet Charity Choir since it started in January 2018.

I live with my husband and two gorgeous children, and love my job as a Speech and Language Therapist, but felt that my life was all about work and family and that I wasn't doing anything for myself. I have always loved singing (mainly in the kitchen while cooking, much to my twelve-year-old son's disgust). However I have a wonderful, vivid memory of singing Carmina Burana at the Royal Albert Hall with my choir on my twelfth birthday.

I had set myself a New Year's resolution to join a choir in January 2018 and by chance a good friend, Kathy, tagged me in a Facebook post about the new Sweet Charity Choir just about to start. We probably both would have chickened out on our own, but together we made the decision to turn up and just haven't looked back.

Singing is such therapy and I genuinely look forward to my Tuesday evenings every week. I have met some great new friends and love the challenge of the fantastic musical arrangements we get to learn very week.

The icing on the cake is when my son greets me at the end of a concert with a huge grin and says "That was amazing, Mum!" Result!

Jane Taylor
Speech and Language Therapist

**Choir Around The Corner**

I first started singing with Jenny in 2011. When I heard she was opening another choir just around the corner from where I live it seemed like too good an opportunity to miss, and I certainly haven't regretted it. Singing certainly lifts the heart, there is no feeling like it, but for me personally, the best part of choir, alongside all the money that we raise for charity and the friendships I have made, is Nick's roulade!!! Fresh cream and chocolate, who could ask for anything more.

Karen Pearson
Printer, Southampton University

**Medicine For The Soul**

I have always enjoyed singing. My mum and dad used to both comment how I hummed all the time when I was younger. Humming was a sign that my spirits were high: everything was right in my little world.

I met one of my best friends at school, at the age of 12. We had a shared love of music and used to spend a lot of our lunch hours at school belting out Alice Cooper tunes or Kate Bush ballads, flicking our long, untrained, permed locks around, imagining we were idolised rock goddesses. That was probably the first time I experienced 'performing' - in front of an involuntary audience who had no choice but to listen to our warbling!

After that, I spent the next few years just belting out my favourite tunes in the car, sometimes alone, sometimes with that involuntary audience again - with the windows open or, for that up close and personal feel, with passengers in the car. I have often been asked to pipe down because I get all the words wrong!

Singing when I was in the shower, singing in the kitchen, whilst cooking, just singing wherever I could.

Then, not long after having my second child (Miles), I decided to have some singing lessons - learning to control my voice a little more and using the correct techniques to 'reach those high notes.' My teacher used to record me and sometimes, when I listened back to it, I could hardly believe it was me!

Wanting to put my new found 'voice' to good use, I joined my local choral society - The Verwood Choral Society - where I enjoyed singing as part of the soprano section and learning a range of songs - from songs from the musicals to Zadok the Priest by

Handel. I found immense pleasure and satisfaction from learning new songs and I really enjoyed the buzz of performing.

Then, one day, in April 2010, my singing stopped. I couldn't sing any more. There was no music in my soul. My dear father, who had been suffering in silence with depression for many years, attempted to end his life, desperate to free from the insomnia and dark thoughts that had been enveloping his mind and his body for many months. He was rushed to the intensive care head injury unit at Southampton Hospital where, as a family, we held vigil around his bedside, whilst he was in a coma, talking to him, writing to him and just willing him to recover.

He did but as he came around, it became clear he was not as thrilled to have survived as we were. It was hard but we never gave up on him. We needed him to know how loved he was and so, at least twice a week, throughout his 4 months of rehab, I took my boys and husband and sat talking around his bed - sometimes to him, sometimes just to each other, depending on his mood.

I gave up choir through this ordeal, however. Of course, it was difficult to find time but oddly, I just could not sing. I couldn't bring myself to do what brought me happiness. I just couldn't do it.

And then my mum was diagnosed with bowel cancer. Still no voice.

My mum and dad both survived and life went on. I started a teacher training year and, my goodness, I barely had time to talk to my lovely (and very supportive) husband and two boys, let alone find the time to sing again! But it's probably exactly what I should have done. It would have lifted me, given me some 'me' time and given me another focus apart from all the assignments, observations, planning and marking that seemed to monopolise that year.

That year ended, I graduated with a distinction, and my husband's world crashed around him. His father died after a severe stroke and his mother (who had been suffering with early onset of Alzheimers) became his responsibility. In the end, heartbreakingly, we made the decision to put her in a dementia care home. It was a difficult decision but really the only one we could make.

So, as you can imagine, the years went by and my voice was still suppressed but gradually my voice 'came back'. The rock star performances in the car, in the shower and in the kitchen returned.

But then, years later, tragedy struck again. After a long battle with bowel cancer, my brother-in law and dear friend (my sister actually met him through me and my husband as we all met at university), Matt, was told that the cancer had metastasised to his liver and he had just 10 months to live. The news was almost unbearable. How could this happen to such a kind, funny and considerate man and his lovely wife and two boys? It felt like someone punching you repeatedly in the stomach until you could hardly breathe, until you were physically sick.

And then I saw it: Juliette Otton's post on Facebook of a video of the Sweet Charity Choir singing Come Alive. It's weird, I'd never really properly gotten to know Juliette. We'd met through a mutual friend a couple of times, we got on (she's also a teacher) and it turned out she lived down the road so we became FB friends and occasionally said hello if we passed in the street. But I truly think we were destined to be friends and best singing buddies.

I contacted Juliette and asked her about the choir: it was local, it was once a month on a weekend - perfect - not a weekly commitment. And they sang modern music! This was it. It felt right. It was 'the one'. I had a feeling in my bones.

So the Sunday of my taster session arrived. I was a bit nervous but also very excited. I'd said so many times over the years that I would return to a choir - now the day had come. We learnt Symphony by Clean Bandit and wow.... I just loved it. Jenny, the Musical Director, was an inspiration. The positivity just emanated deep from within her and rubbed off onto every single person there. Plus, I learnt a whole song really well, ate cake, drank tea and chatted to a lot of new people - just fabulous. I came home singing and smiling. My husband commented on what a difference it had made to my mood, which had been quite 'heavy', as we were all so deeply affected by the news of our lovely Matt.

I remember one Sunday - Rob's mum (who was now in the late stages of dementia) was going to pass imminently (a blessing and a

127

relief in many ways but so sad and poignant, at the same time, because the seven 'lost years' suddenly became so apparent) and Matt's health and taken a downward turn. I was sat on the sofa; I could barely move. I just felt so down and so heavy-hearted. I almost decided not to go to choir but my husband persuaded me to go.

And he was so right: yes, I do get emotional when I sing but it always seems to produce the 'happy' hormones in my body and I always feel lifted and lighter (mentally - not physically - unfortunately!). I knew, after that, that it was imperative that I go to every single rehearsal I could manage. And it proved to be the right decision.

Over the next couple months, not only did my mother-in-law pass over but so did Matt, leaving behind so much love. Gosh, grief is so hard. It's like being in a dark bubble. Life seemingly goes on as normal but inside you just feel so flat and, well, 'dead'. On top of feeling like this, work was also stressful at this time: I am a teacher and the pressure at school was unbelievable at times. With life at home so stressful and work so pressurised, I sometimes felt so 'on the edge' - like I could literally explode at any moment!

That's when a work colleague suggested to me that I walk to work, get some fresh air and just 'notice' what is around me. So that's what I started doing. And guess what I listened to as I walked? Jenny's beautiful soprano voice, singing the parts I needed to learn for the Christmas concert. I loved it. I almost burst into song just walking along the pavement to school. And I learnt every song - word perfect. This small change to my routine helped. It really helped. Once again, SCC at the heart of my well-being.

Thankfully, gradually, the bubble got lighter and I felt able to truly smile again. The sadness and loss never goes - it returns, at times, like a punch in the stomach, winding you and throwing you completely off course - but I felt able to enjoy life again, slowly.

I truly believe that this period of darkness, pain and grief would have been so much more difficult without the Sweet Charity Choir. It was like a medicine for the soul.

Apart from helping me through some unbearable times, the

choir has pushed me completely out of my comfort zone at times. I've always loved performing: I get nervous but I find it such an emotional and spiritual experience. I often feel like I could literally 'burst into tears' at any point but, gosh, the buzz I get from it is unreal. In January 2019, Jenny invited us to busk in London on the Southbank. What an experience! Something I never thought I'd do but it was such a 'different' experience - I felt such a sense of achievement that day and I am already looking forward to when we next do it. The members of the choir are extraordinarily passionate and committed and it truly is a privilege to be associated with them.

Thank you Sweet Charity Choir - for your excitement, your loyalty and, of course, your voices.

Katy Anderson
Teacher


## Strength In Numbers

From as young as I can remember my sisters and I put on singing shows for aunties and uncles. We would appear from behind the heavy curtains that hung in the "Front Room" and perform songs from the Sound of Music or Liza Minnelli (a family favourite). No solos, just pure group performance, we became known as the "Second Nolan sisters". I can remember standing under a makeshift spotlight belting out the high notes without a care in the world. But then puberty and self-doubt set in and it all faded.

I had always had aspirations of being a singer and admired the entertainers at Butlins and Pontins. I briefly made enquiries to sing on a cruise liner too; I am sure if I'd had that one friend who was like minded I would have found the courage to have done it, but alas my career headed in a different direction. It wasn't until many years later when I had married that my sister and I rekindled a little bit of our showman days and sang the entire repertoire of South Pacific to my (then) husband's family...only to be told to pipe down and that I couldn't sing...I was defeated. We parted!

Let's roll the years forward to 2011. I saw an advertisement to join a taster session for a new modern choir starting in Leigh on Sea. Excited, my sister and I decided to give it a go. She never made the taster session, but I did and by the end of the session I was singing "I knew you were waiting" …. An actual song and we sounded great. I have never looked back.

But that's not my story. My story is what has happened since then….

The Leigh Choir started with just a handful of friendly people, who, like me, loved to sing. I made new friends, which made me keep going. Little did I know just what those friendships would mean to me. It's funny how you are drawn to people, all different but with something in tune with yourself. As the choir grew so my circle of friends grew with it. First we arranged a meal out at Christmas, then we met for lunch before or after a gig. This developed into birthdays, weddings or even 'just because' meet ups. These friends became important to me and supported me through some of the more difficult times in my life, like the death of my mum or my son's relationship break up.

So strong is our group friendship that in 2016 we all decided to go away together. 12 in total rented a house. It was so much fun, we did it again in 2017, 14 this time, 2018, 15 and in 2019 16. We call ourselves the Big Weekenders (BW's for short) and each brings something different to our weekends. I am the party planner and have got the ladies doing all manner of things like playing obscure instruments (little did they know until their group performance that individually they had all been learning the same song) Cheerleading or Sunday night at the Lyndon Palladium (Lyndon was the name of the house we stayed in). Putting on an act for our entertainment, we had everything from a Hoedown, Glam Rock, Songs of our Summers and even a duet of Michael Jackson's Thriller including the dance…watch out ladies, BW 2019 is fast approaching.

So let's move forward. Alas in 2017 my first choir had to close so I was choir-less for a few months, During this time I had convinced myself that I didn't need to go to choir, I could manage without it, save the money, do something else, a bit like trying to cope without your regular medication. I would never have believed that I could become so down and once again so full of self-doubting. I hadn't realised just what singing meant and I was missing the buzz I got from my rehearsals and from seeing my friends every week.

My second husband, Steve, noticed my enthusiasm was flagging too, and said that I should find another choir. I think he was secretly missing my impromptu kitchen rehearsal, or trying to sing my harmonies to a song on the radio! Some of my friends had joined a new Choir in Southend so I decided to give it a go. Hoorah, Sweet Charity you saved me. I was re awoken, it didn't take me long to bounce back, and my BW's were back by my side. I felt like I was home again and we are just as strong as ever. My husband is very supportive of my singing and loves my new girl friends, his encouragement has manifested itself many times. He attends gigs and puts up with my endless practicing but the biggest thing he has done for me without me knowing is secretly paid for me to go to New York to sing at Carnegie Hall in July this year!

I love my husband, I love my BW's, I love Sweet Charity Choir. I love to sing (but not on my own); as an individual I am weak, but with the support of my family and with my friends by my side I am strong ... very strong.

Lynn Gunter

## Music Over The Years ...From Poole To Carnegie Hall

Music has always been my first love, having started to learn the recorder at six, then to sing and play the trombone from the age of eight. In 1979 my sister and I stood in the front row of the first combined school performance of 'Joseph and His Technicolour Dream Coat' at The Light House in Poole! I took part in three band tours of Cornwall with the junior school and I was one of the first five girls to join the boy's Senior School Brass Band. I also sang in the church choir.

In my twenties and early thirties, I learnt to play the baritone in a brass band, performing at lots of concerts and contests throughout the country.

In my early forties, I rediscovered singing again and it was something that I did for myself. (my 'me' time!) In January 2017, I had the pleasure of joining Sweet Charity Choir. There is nothing better than spending a Sunday afternoon with likeminded people, singing, eating lovely homemade cake and raising money for great causes.

As I turned fifty last year I thought I would like to mark the special year with a trip to New York. Then thanks to our Come Alive Video going viral in 2018 we were invited to sing in 'Carnegie Hall', New York, on the 15 July 2019, which is so amazing and exciting, bring it on!

By singing my voice has grown stronger and it has definitely helped with my breathing. Whilst I am singing, there is no time to think of anything else apart from being in that moment and I always leave a rehearsal happy with my endorphins full to the brim ready to carry me through the week ahead.

I would like to take this opportunity, to thank Jenny for sharing her talent and enthusiasm for music with us. Long may it continue...

Sue Divall

* * *

Music has been a mainstay in my life for as long as I can remember. Piano lessons were at the centre of my childhood relationship with my Nanna, the main piano teacher in town; she was a performing musician and singer in her time, and ran a music school with her mother. I remember she had an eclectic collection of instruments, the most intriguing of which were the 'sleigh bells'. I can't remember NOT being able to play the piano, lessons started at such an early age. I loved singing in the school choir and went on to learn the oboe at 'Saturday Music School', where I further learned the art of making music with others in the orchestra and a woodwind ensemble. I've always felt playing an instrument or singing to be therapeutic, a form of escapism.

Strangely enough, my husband's grandfather was also a piano teacher, and it is a delight to witness music coursing through the veins of our children. Our eleven year old daughter can play by ear which leaves me in total awe, and it is such a pleasure to see her face light up as she masters her first songwriting project. She's the opposite of me, in that she will only play if she has an audience! Our nine year old son loves to listen to music and is becoming quite the oracle; he curls himself around his CD player (yes, retro!) and indulges in everything from Bowie to Bon Jovi, Crowded House to Drake. He sings in the school choir with the sons of my Sweet Charity Choir buddies Jane and Kathy, although he wishes it was a rock choir!

Music plays an important role in my work life as a speech therapist. I work with adults with neurological conditions, such as Stroke, Parkinson's Disease, Multiple Sclerosis and Motor Neurone Disease. Evidence to support the use of music in neurorehabilitation continues to grow, and I'm proud to have contributed to this research base, having explored the relationship between 'musicianship' and the ability to interpret intonation patterns in speech. When working on the Stroke Unit at Southend Hospital, I introduced a music group. Particularly for a condition called 'apraxia of speech', music can tap into automaticity in the brain, bridging the 'gap' between the right hemisphere and the left, 'freeing' up the words. One man I treated was only able to say "well, well, well" following a Stroke but during a music group he was able to sing the whole of 'Happy Birthday' to his wife! This confirmed to me that music is magic.

When Jane and Kathy mentioned Sweet Charity Choir to me, I leapt at the chance to bring music back into my life again. As I'm sure many can relate to, it is a busy time of life with young children, and everything seems to revolve around them – it is so lovely to have that precious Tuesday evening doing something for me. Coincidentally, I joined the choir at a time when I suddenly became a carer for a close family member who was going through an acute mental health crisis. The choir really did serve as an escape, and it seemed very timely that I was welcomed into this supportive and friendly group that gives so much to mental health (and other) charities. I just know that, however I'm feeling at the start of a rehearsal, I will leave feeling energised and joyful.

Anna Allen
Speech and Language Therapist

\* \* \*

I've spent most of my life thinking that I couldn't sing at all. I admit I'm not a strong singer and certainly I wouldn't sing a solo, but I know that I am able to hold a tune and can sing very high which I think really helps sometimes, when other people can't.

I used to do mediaeval re-enactment in a group called the Lion Rampant, where I would dress up as a medieval lady, ride horses in the skill-at-arms, sword-fight, dance, and play the recorder. There was also a choir in the group, which my husband Mark joined but I never did, still believing then that I couldn't sing. During that time, a music teacher joined the group and told me that if I could play the recorder and read music then she was sure I could sing. She sat down with me one afternoon and convinced me that I could sing soprano. Feeling more confident in my ability, I joined the mediaeval choir, and really enjoyed singing in the shows.

One of my friends is a member of Amersham Acapella, a competition choir and gold medallists in ladies' barbershop. I tried out for them and got through the first stage but unfortunately not the second, as they were such a high standard and I really wasn't good enough.

However, I had discovered a real love for singing and wanted to find somewhere that I could sing regularly. Somebody at Amersham Acapella suggested I joined Rock Choir and told me what good fun it was. I joined the Wokingham Rock Choir with some ladies from work for a couple of years and really enjoyed my time there. Subsequently, when I moved to Bournemouth, I thought it would be a good idea to join the Bournemouth Rock Choir as I didn't know anybody at all, and I knew it was a great way of meeting people, as well as being able to continue singing.

The year before, I had been to the NEC for a nationwide Rock Choir event with my Wokingham choir and I remember Jenny had written a beautiful arrangement for the Rock Choir leaders to sing. Subsequently, when I was looking up the details of the Bournemouth choir on the internet I was absolutely delighted to see it was Jenny who was the leader. However, by the time I joined, Jenny had already left which was a shame, but I joined anyway and absolutely loved it. The new leader, Chris, is lovely. The Bournemouth choir members were so friendly and not long after joining I had the fantastic opportunity of going to Barcelona with the choir, where I got to socialise with other members, and a few of the ladies in the bass section took me under their wing.

Of course, when I heard about Sweet Charity, I didn't hesitate to join and I went along to the very first rehearsal. I was hooked immediately. Jenny's arrangements are fantastic and she is such a talented musician. I also love that she provides the music as well as the lyrics as it makes it so much easier for me to learn new songs, some of which I haven't even heard of because they are more my sons' generation than mine. I would never have listened to them were it not for Jenny and Sweet Charity. She has introduced me to a whole range of new music that I hadn't previously known, but now really enjoy.

While living in Bournemouth, I was caring for my Auntie Joyce, who had Alzheimer's. She was deteriorating and I had to put her into a care home, which cost about a thousand pounds a week. Her money soon ran out but she was so settled that I didn't want to move her. I knew I needed a job that earned the kind of money where I could afford to pay for her care. The only one suitable that came up was based in the Middle East. I was offered the job on a two-year contract in January, but then sadly Auntie Joyce died in the February. I made the decision to go ahead with the job anyway as it was a great opportunity, which I may have regretted not taking.

So now I am living in Dubai, and missing Sweet Charity enormously. Jenny is happy for me to remain a member, and just get to rehearsals whenever I am home. I am learning the new songs from the Dropbox, and practising every day in my car while I drive to work and back. It's not ideal, as I miss Jenny's input, but I am doing my best. I recently attended a rehearsal where we practised Bring Him Home, which is the most wonderful arrangement, and which had many choir members in tears. I was happy to find that I was able to sing along with the choir with no problems. I will be going to New York in the summer to sing at Carnegie Hall and I am so excited. With Jenny's help and guidance on the night, I know I'll be fine.

Den Carroll
School Manager/Academic Advisor

## My Happy Place

I saw a Facebook ad for a brand new choir during the Christmas period. I needed to find something just for me. Caring for a mum with Alzheimer's and two teenage boys is quite hard going sometimes and I wanted a choir where I would fit in and not have the pressure of an audition.

Within five minutes of walking into the choir hall, I was chatting to two fellow sopranos who were equally terrified. Then along came Jenny! Quite possibly one of the most amazing people I've ever met. Choir means so much to me, it's my escapism and my happy place and I have made so many wonderful and caring friends.

Nicky Radziusz

## Elgar To Elvis

I have loved music all my life though I never learned to play an instrument beyond a few chords on an acoustic guitar. To this day I wish I'd learned drum-kit!

Different times of one's life are characterised by the music of the time and can evoke memories that are both happy and painful. I believe music has the power to create and modify mood. My taste in music has always been broad, from middle of the road pop to heavy metal, Elvis, Stones, Beatles, Petshop Boys, Trance, Abba, Bucks Fizz, Rachmaninov, Led Zeppelin, Leonard Cohen, Tchaikovsky, Elgar, Einaudi, Joni Mitchell, Carol King to name but a few. My favourite instruments are the cello and the piano. I am aware of a musical matrix which has held me together many times when life has seemed difficult.

Singing for me began at about 8 years old when I joined the local church choir where my father sang bass and my brother was a boy soprano. The choir master, an ex-docker and black belt in judo from Liverpool, aroused in me a deep passion for the sense of connection that singing in a choir can generate. He also taught me how to breathe. By the time I was 12, I had sung several classical pieces including the Messiah, the Crucifixion and Faure's Requiem.

I left home at 18, my career choice to study drama having been crushed. Sadly, I didn't sing again until I was nearly 60 but when the chance came to sing pop classics in a choir I jumped at it. It has not disappointed me: the friendships, the camaraderie, the love; they are genuine. At every rehearsal, we are all in a beautiful creative moment together.

To my horror, a year ago I was diagnosed with a potentially life-threatening condition when a tumour was found in my right lung, during a scan on my heart. It was the size of a large marble but nothing was known of its type or malevolence. The Doctors could neither agree on a diagnosis nor the method of management initially which was pretty unnerving.

The normality and routine of being in a choir at this time kept me stable during a year of being scanned and x-rayed and eventually the decision was made to operate and last Autumn I underwent surgery to remove a lobe (the second largest) of my right lung. It was explained to me that my voice might be affected (eeeeek!!) and that **my** contribution to my recovery was paramount so I got on an exercise bike 2 days after the operation to re-inflate what was left of my right lung. The 'battle' to get back had started. Four weeks after surgery I came back to choir and hummed my way through

Wonderful World and received many hugs from well-wishers. It was a place I felt safe and cared for.

Although I've been told I'll always be breathless I know that singing and the deep controlled breathing it requires, has aided my recovery. Interestingly my experience has enabled me to talk to other people 'going through it' in the choir. I feel a deep respect for them. They are people who just won't lie down but sing their way through adversity.

The benefits of being part of Sweet Charity Choir are for me life affirming.

Sally Phillips
Retired


**Sharing The Joy**

I was a Director of Music for 40 years and am now retired.

As I look back over that time I continue to believe that music has always been one of the most powerful experiences we can offer our children. It brings inclusion to an outsider; it brings release to tension and stress; it gives a sense of purpose to a child that is 'lost' and it raises self esteem.

My music room was a sanctuary – I encouraged and actively endorsed that concept throughout my career. In my music room we were equals, sharing a common purpose of making music, sharing its joy both amongst ourselves at practices and with others in performance. Music was all inclusive – there was a place for everyone regardless of age or ability. We strove for excellence, won competitions, sang with Westlife, travelled abroad and made lasting memories.

As teachers, we often don't realise the impact we have on the children we teach - classes come and go, different schools and different countries – you forget the names BUT they don't forget you! I was once told by an ex pupil, now a mum, I saved her life! Another pupil is a Head of Music herself and paying it forward. And now I'm on the other side of the fence I'm discovering for myself the joy of Sweet Charity, just as I hope my pupils did.

We, as parents, grandparents, friends and family, must not take any of this for granted and become complacent. We must ensure that music remains in the school curriculum, that children have the same opportunities we had because if we don't, where will our future orchestras, musicians and choirs come from? And a world without music is just unimaginable.

Christine Petherick
Director of Music

## What Singing And Music Means To Me

"Turns a crappy day into a happy day."
Maggie Bracher

"I suffer with depression and I listen to music (all genres) to help lift my mood."
Jan Solecki

"Joy."
Shirley Kavanagh

"It's a happy release – a pleasure – and very healing."
Chris Noonan

"Lovely people."
Anon

"I feel I 'belong' when singing with the choir. I've always loved singing, especially in harmony."
Jan Solecki

"Unfailingly lifts my spirits, no matter what else is going on in my life. I also love the spectacle of Jenny coming up with innovative teaching tools."

Katherine Robertson

"I suffer with depression and singing is my therapy. It is 2 hours a week where I don't think about crying but learning and singing!!."
Anon

"My Dad was a music teacher, church organist and choir master. From as far back as I can remember I sat in the wings or on an organ bench or even got to sing with the big kids! My Mum took part too so we were always singing show tunes. Music has always been a big part of my life."
Kath

"My happy place."
Sally Phillips

"Singing is a release of pressure and an outpouring of joy!."
Chris Petherel

"To me, it makes me feel relaxed."
Anon

"Friendship, team work, shared emotions."
Chris Petherel

"Music starts my day, envelops my family and keeps us all going!."
Ann Wright

"A sense of camaraderie, uplifting times, makes you forget your worries for a little while."
Chris Noonan

"Makes me happy."
Anon

"Can be totally uplifting – I go into a session and sometimes come out a different person – pure natural adrenaline rush!"
Tracey Newman

"Gets out my feelings."
Anon

From members of the Soprano section

# Interval

# Take A Break With

# Some Choir Cuisine

Verjizzle Ma Drizzle

Today's a day for bountiful bakes
Savouries, biscuits and handmade cakes
The judging of 2 resplendent lemon drizzles
Sweet and crunchy and tongue tingling fizzles
A Singathon lasting all the day
I'm sure we'll leave Greyfriars in a different way
We started all bushy tailed and bright eyed
Ready to sing our songs with pride
Jenny gave us the New York schmooze
In her stylish and comfy tartan shoes
Pointing out our mistakes, we need to get it right
When we sing our concert on that Manhattan Monday night
But she does it with warmth, humour and grace
And usually with a funny face
We're Sweet Charity Choir, practising and having a ball
Getting ready for New Yorks Carnegie Hall
But as our battery starts to run down
Jenny's face showed a humorous frown
'Hey' shouted Colin showing his singing prowess
He cracks me up I must confess
Jenny shouts back about the arrangement she wrote

'Now sing it in the right note'
We did some recording with mic's up high
George fiddled with it, I'm not sure why
But I wasn't disappointed cos he was dressed to the nines
And reaching up he flashed his Calvin Kleins
A bit of heckling saw him blush
We've all got a huge Gorgeous George crush
Kelly came to take a look
And gather info for the book
About the choir, the history and effect
Funny tales and stories, I expect
There was Easter treats, pens, songbooks, CD's as well
And we sang songs about the Teen Spirit Smell
Shine with a few solos but none were pre planned
While the tea ladies kept the tea station manned
Fuel for the warblers to keep us going
And cake of course to keep us crowing
We all pulled up a comfy chair
And each time we sat escaped a wisp of air
Sounding like a fart en masse
A steady escape of a compressed gas
Our rehearsals are always filled with so much fun
Moments of laughter for everyone
But our mission is to help those that are in need
Of every colour and every creed
A wonderful bunch of people who inspire
We are Sweet Charity Choir

Jilly Firmin

* * *

My name is Cheryl from Southend and my favourite things in life are cake and music so being in Jenny Deacon's Sweet Charity choir is perfect for me! I joined the choir when it started in January 2018. I went along for a 'taster' with a few of my friends and family to see what it was all about and we haven't looked back! I enjoy simple baking that isn't too time consuming because I'm no expert. I mainly do it for fun and enjoyment and the kind donations from our members helps to raise money for our chosen charities.

My daughter has been vegan for about 5 years now (as are a couple of other choir members) so I thought if I bake vegan as well as regular no one misses out on treats! Here's a couple of easy to make vegan recipes (but not just for vegans!) I've tried both recipes many times and they always go down well with our 'Southenders'

### Easy Vegan Chocolate Brownies

### Ingredients

9 x13 tin ( greased and lined)
250g plain flour
350g demerara sugar
65g plain cocoa powder
1tsp salt
250ml water
250ml vegetable oil (or similar)
2tsp vanilla extract
(You can stop here or add anything below)
Optional extras to mix in the batter choose a couple
150g dark chocolate
150g Glacier cherries (chopped and washed or they sink)
Grated zest of orange & 1tbsp juice
150g Sultanas
150g Mixed nuts
150g Smashed Oreos
Crunchy Peanut butter (2-3 table spoons)

## Method

Pre heat oven fan 180/ gas 4 approx 25 - 30mins
Mix together in a large bowl flour, sugar, cocoa powder and salt.
Add water,oil,vanilla extract mix well until blended, pour evenly into tin.
Bake approx 25 - 30mins check if you want less gooey bake a little longer (if so cover with foil so top doesnt get too done)
Leave to cool cut into squares.

Cheryl Say

## Vegan Peanut butter cookies

## Ingredients

22 lined baking trays
25g plain flour
1tsp baking soda
1/2 tsp salt
1/2 tsp ground nutmeg
110g dairy free margarine ( eg vitalite / pure)
150g caster sugar
150g soft brown sugar
1tsp ground flax seed
3 tbsp water
175g- 200g peanut butter smooth or crunchy
Demerara sugar (for rolling)

## Method

Pre heat oven fan 160 / gas 4
Combine flax seed with 2 tbsp water set aside
In an electric mixing bowl add dairy free margarine and sugar beat until fluffy approx 3 minutes , add flax mixture and vanilla, beat 2 minutes then add peanut butter mix until combined.

In another bowl combine flour, baking soda, salt and nutmeg
Add dry ingredients to wet and mix only until just combined cover and place dough in fridge to chill for 10 - 15 mins
Pre heat oven
In a bowl place demerara sugar
Roll a tablespoon of dough between your palms and roll into a ball then roll in the sugar place ball on lined baking tin and press down with a fork place all cookies 1.5' apart
Bake approx 10 - 12 minutes leave to cool on tray for 5 mins transfer to cooling rack.

Cheryl Say

## Dorset Apple Traybake

appx 16 cake squares

### Ingredients

450g cooking apples (ie Bramleys)
Juice of ½ lemon
225g butter, softened
280g golden caster sugar
4 eggs
2 tsp vanilla extract
350g self-raising flour
2 tsps baking powder
Demerara sugar, to sprinkle

### Method

Heat oven to 180C/fan 160C/gas4. Butter and line a rectangular baking tin (approx. 27cm x 20cm) with parchment paper. Peel, core and thinly slice the apples then squeeze the lemon juice over. Set to one side.
Place the butter, caster sugar, eggs, vanilla, flour and baking

powder into a large bowl and mix well until smooth. Spread half the mixture into the prepared tin. Arrange half the apples over the top of the mixture, then repeat the layers. Sprinkle over the demerara sugar. Then bake for 45-50 mins until golden and springy to the touch. Leave to cool for 10mins, then turn out of the tin and remove paper. Cut into bars or squares.

Christine Hensser

## Nick's Chocolate Roulade Recipe

This one seems to be a favourite with Sweet Charity Choir members. There are lots of recipes for the same cake out there in cyber land but this is based on Mary Berry's. It is a slightly more technically challenging recipe but like favourite dishes, you get to know all the ingredients and quantities and don't have to refer to the recipe. This one for me is easy to remember for the cake mix as it reminds me of "The Beast" and his number 666! As I'm a bit long in the tooth I tend to use Imperial quantities and so to help younger people I will of course include that new-fangled metric system!

**Ingredients Cake mix**

6 eggs
6 ozs (170gms) caster sugar
6ozs (170gms) chocolate
2 tablespoons cocoa powder

**Filling**

10 floz (300ml) double cream
You can add some rum or brandy to the cream to give it a bit of a
kick if you so wish.

**Optional**

You can add fruit like raspberries, cherries or strawberries as you
roll the roulade.

**Method**

Preheat the oven to 180C/fan 160C/gas 4. Lightly grease a 13in x
9in (33cm x 23cm) swiss-roll tin and line with non-stick baking
parchment, cut a slit at each corner to fit parchment neatly in the
corner of the tray.
Break the chocolate into small pieces over a bowl and stand the
bowl over a pan of hot water; the bowl must not touch the water or
the chocolate may overheat. Place the pan over a low heat until the
chocolate has melted.
Crack the eggs and split the egg white and yolks into separate large
bowls, the yolks going in with the measured sugar. (Cook's tip, if
you get eggshell in the bowl, use one half of the empty eggshell
case to pick it out)
First, whisk the egg whites until stiff but not dry. Can tip the bowl
upside down if you feel confident to do so and the white should stay
there (you hope!)
Then using the whisk (its okay to do it this way, you don't need to

148

clean them off of the egg white but don't do it the other way round as the egg yolk would stop the white from stiffening up), whisk until you have a light and creamy consistency. It will be a pale creamy yellow in appearance.

Add the cooled chocolate and fold until evenly blended, it will be quite thick and gooey.

Stir a couple of large spoonfuls (I use a large vegetable serving spoon for this) of the egg whites into the chocolate mixture. Mix gently, this will loosen up the mixture then fold in the remaining egg whites, suggest a figure of 8 action and finally lightly fold in the sieved cocoa powder. Only do this a few times you don't want to fully mix it with the rest.

Spread evenly in the prepared tin. Give the tin a gentle sideways shake to even the mix in the tray. Bake in the preheated oven for about 20 minutes until firm. Don't worry it will crack, that's to be expected.

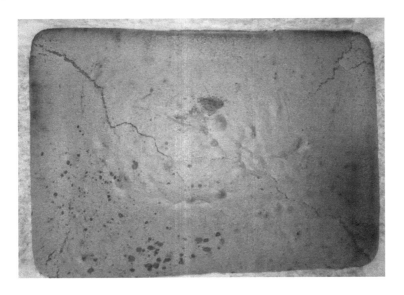

**Cake just after removal from oven to illustrate cracking.**

Remove the cake from the oven, leave in the tin, some recipes say cover with a dry tea towel and leave until cold, I just let it cool down but not necessarily cold if in a rush, once the tray is cool enough I would then turn out the roulade as the next step but do ensure it has fully cooled before spreading cream.

Whip the cream until it just holds its shape and dust a large piece of greaseproof paper with sifted icing sugar. Turn out the roulade and peel off the paper. Spread with the cream evenly and go up to the edges so that those with the end don't miss out! Score a mark about an inch (2.5cm) in along the short edge, then roll up very tightly like a swiss roll, using the paper to help. What I do to help is place my other hand along the opposite short edge to stop the roulade moving as I pull the parchment towards it to roll it up. Sometimes I will stop and press down on the roll just to make it firmer.

Do not worry when the roulade cracks – a good one should! Dust with more sifted icing sugar to serve. Enjoy!

Nick McCullen

## Summer Pudding

### Ingredients

Serves 6-8
900g loaf tin
500g frozen or fresh berries (include blackcurrants or blackberries for colour)
135g blackcurrant or strawberry jelly block
12 slices day-old white bread (approx.)
Fresh fruit and cream to serve
If making for adults only a slug of fruit liqueur (eg sloe gin) added to the cooked fruit gives an extra oomph!

### Method

Prepare tin by greasing inside and lining with cling film, leaving enough overhang to cover.
Defrost frozen fruit gently in a pan with a tablespoon of water or simmer fresh fruit until just soft and juices running. Add sugar to taste.

Meanwhile dissolve the jelly in a little boiling water, then add to the fruit. Mix in gently.

Cut the crusts off the bread and trim to fit the base, sides and end of the tin.

Dip the slices in the fruit juice. Line the tin.

Tip the fruit into the tin and cover with more bread slices.

Bring the clingfilm up and over the top to cover and place a weight (eg soup can) on top.

Leave to set in the fridge for as long as possible – ideally overnight. When ready to serve, lift the pudding out of the tin using the clingfilm, and invert on to your serving platter. Decorate with fresh fruit and serve with cream or icecream (or both!)

This makes an easy and attractive summer party dessert.

(My version of an old favourite)

Georgie Foord

## Chocolate Cupcakes:

## Ingredients

50 grams unsweetened cocoa powder 240 ml boiling hot water
175 grams SR flour
1 teaspoon baking powder
1/4 teaspoon baking soda
1/2 teaspoon salt
113 grams unsalted butter, at room temperature
200 grams granulated white sugar
2 teaspoons vanilla extract
2 large eggs, at room temperature

## Chocolate Fudge Frosting:

115 grams unsweetened chocolate, coarsely chopped
150 grams unsalted butter, at room temperature
160 grams icing sugar, sifted
1 1/2 teaspoons vanilla extract

**Method**

Preheat your oven to 350 degrees F (180 degrees C). Put paper cases in fairy cake tins.

In a small bowl, stir the unsweetened cocoa powder with the boiling hot water until smooth. Let cool to room temperature.

In another bowl, whisk or sift the flour with the baking powder, baking soda, and salt.

Then in the bowl of your electric mixer, fitted with the paddle attachment, beat the butter until smooth. Add the sugar and vanilla extract and beat on medium high speed until light and fluffy. Add the eggs one at a time, beating until fully incorporated. Scrape down the sides and bottom of the bowl as needed. Add the flour mix and then the cocoa mixture. Beat only until the ingredients are incorporated. Do not overbeat at this stage .

Fill each muffin cup about 3/4 full with batter and bake for about 18-20 minutes or until risen, springy to the touch. Do not over bake or the cupcakes will be dry. Remove from oven and place on a wire rack to cool. Once the cupcakes have completely cooled, pipe with the Chocolate Frosting. Decorate with chocolate button or sprinkles.

Jilly Firmin

**Easy Peasy Lemon Squeezy Cheesecake.**

**Ingredients**

2 packets of ginger nut biscuits
4oz butter
600mls double cream
340 grms Philadelphia cheese
3oz castor sugar
5 unwaxed lemons (grated peel and juice)

**Method**

Crush biscuits pour over melted butter, mix and use to line base of deep dish or loose based cake tin (aprox 7 inch)
Whisk cream until it reaches the ribbon stage, do not over whisk at this stage.
Add cream, grated lemon peel and castor sugar. Mix gently with the cream.
Squeeze lemons and add to the cream mixture. Beat slowly until it forms a thick but smooth mixture.
Place on top of biscuit crumb
I decorate with sliced Kiwi but this is optional
Chill for at least 3 hours

Debbie Mantle


**Dorset Apple Cake**

**Ingredients**

225g self raising flour
110g butter or marg
110g caster sugar
225g cooking apples, peeled, cored and diced
Grated rind of 1 lemon
1 medium egg
50g sultanas
½ teaspoon almond essence (optional)

**Method**

Preheat oven to Gas mark 5, 190°C, 375°F and grease a 20cm, 8 inch round cake tin.
Rub butter into the flour in a large bowl until it resembles breadcrumbs

Stir in the sugar, apples, lemon rind, and egg and mix well
Add sultanas
Pour into tin and bake 30-40 mins until golden

Karen Whitty

## Oreo Cupcake

Makes 12-15

**Ingredients**

**Cupcakes**

170g light brown caster sugar
170g unsalted butter, softened
3 eggs, whisked

170g self-raising flour, sieved
1 tsp baking powder
1 tsp espresso coffee
2 tsp vegetable oil
Packet of Oreo Biscuits

## Topping

60g unsalted butter, softened
60g soft cream cheese
120g icing sugar, sieved
1tsp vanilla extract
Up to 1tbs milk

## Method

## Cupcakes

Take the Oreo biscuits and separate them, placing the side with the cream faced up in the muffin case.
With the other half of the Oreo put into a plastic bag and crush until crumbs
Preheat oven to 180 C
In a large bowl cream together the caster sugar and butter until light and fluffy
Add eggs, and whisk until mixed
Fold flour and baking powder into mixture until creamy
Add expresso coffee and oil until mixed
Spoon the mixture into muffin cases until approx. 2 thirds full
Bake in the pre heated oven for 20-22 minutes until they spring back when lightly touched
Remove from baking tray and cool

## Buttercream Topping

Whisk the butter until pale in colour then add the cream cheese
Gradually add the icing sugar until all blended, light and creamy

Add the crushed Oreo biscuits
Add vanilla extract and a little milk to the mixture and whisk.
Adding a little more milk if needed
Pipe the buttercream topping onto the cakes and decorate.

Emma and Sue Brooks

## Chocolate Chip Cookies

**Ingredients**

100g butter
100g dark soft brown sugar
50g light soft brown sugar
1 egg, beaten
100g wholemeal self raising flour
100g plain flour
100g chocolate chips

**Method**

Preheat oven 180°C, gas mark 4 and grease 2 baking trays
Cream butter and sugars together until very light and fluffy
Beat in the egg
Stir in flours and chocolate chips
Divide mixture into walnut size pieces by rolling between hands
Place on baking sheets with space to spread out as they cook
Bake 10 mins

Karen Whitty

## Gluten Free Millionaires Shortbread

Having a daughter who follows a gluten free diet I am always
looking out for good recipes that she approves of. I'm happy to say
that she definitely enjoyed this one and when I took some to a

Sweet Charity rehearsal it's safe to say that it was a big hit with everyone there too!

Makes about 40 pieces

**Ingredients**

**Shortbread**

225g butter
110g sugar (I used caster sugar)
350g gluten-free self-raising flour

**Caramel**

225g butter
240g sugar
4 tbsp golden syrup
1 tin/400g sweetened condensed milk

**Topping**

300g chocolate (dark, milk, white or a mix)

**Method**

Preheat oven to 180C/160 fan/ gas 4
Cut the butter into cubes and mix with the sugar (in a food processor) mix until creamy
Next add the flour and mix until it makes a dough. Use hands to bind it together, it's easier
Press into a large greased and lined tray (40x30cms) and prick with a fork all over
Bake for 15/20 mins until golden
Leave to cool in the tin
To make the caramel put the sugar, butter, syrup and condensed

milk in a pan on a low heat and stir until
dissolved.

Then turn up the heat and boil mixture for 3-4 minutes, stirring all the time to prevent it from
catching. Be careful not to let it burn at this stage. It should thicken. (If you like you can test to see if it's
the right consistency by dropping a small amount into a glass of cold water - the caramel will form a
small blob and still be soft.

Pour over the cooled base and leave to cool to set. This will take about an hour.

Once the caramel has set, melt the chocolate and pour over the caramel.

Leave to set. This will take at least an hour

Once set if you put it in the fridge for longer it'll make the block really hard and easier to cut up.

Cut into at least 40 pieces.

They will last about a week if stored in an airtight container.

A tip for getting the shortbread out of the tin easier is by making sure your baking parchment is bigger
than the tin so you can use it to pull the shortbread out.

Kym Mason

## Carrot Cake

### Ingredients

6 fluid oz corn oil/sunflower oil
6 oz caster sugar
6 oz plain flour
8 oz carrots – grated
3 eggs
1 teaspoon vanilla extract
1 teaspoon baking powder
1 teaspoon bicarb of soda

1 teaspoon cinnamon
4 oz chopped walnuts or pecans

## Method

Put all ingredients – except the walnuts/pecans into food processor
and mix thoroughly
Stir in walnuts
Put mixture into a lined 8/9″ deep cake tin and bake in centre of
oven 160°C for approx 1 hr or until skewer inserted into cake comes
out clean

## Icing

## Ingredients

4 oz cream cheese(don't use "skinny" cream cheese, the icing will
end up too sloppy)
2 oz butter
10 oz icing sugar
1 teaspoon vanilla extract

## Method

Mix all of above together, slap onto cake – and enjoy!!

Sue Carter

## Waffle Berry Pudding

## Ingredients

2 packets (200 g each) (sweet) waffles
150 g white chocolate
300 g frozen raspberries
55 g caster sugar

1 tablespoon plain flour
500 ml soured cream or crème fraîche
3 eggs
1/2 teaspoon vanilla extract
1 tablespoon icing sugar
Vanilla ice cream, to serve (optional)

**Method**

Preheat oven to 200°C/fan 180°C/Gas 6. Cut waffles into 2.5-cm pieces; set aside.

Coarsely chop white chocolate. Place half of the waffle pieces into dish. Sprinkle with half of the chopped white chocolate and half of the raspberries; repeat layers with remaining waffle pieces, chopped white chocolate and raspberries.

Place dish in Microwave, uncovered, on HIGH about 3 minutes or until raspberries are defrosted.

Combine caster sugar and flour in bowl; add soured cream, eggs and vanilla extract. Whisk until well blended. Spoon mixture evenly over top of raspberries.

Bake about 30 minutes or until golden brown and set in centre. Remove from oven; cool 10 minutes. Sprinkle with sifted icing sugar. Serve with vanilla ice cream, if desired.

Sue Carter

### Suzie's Chocolate Truffles

**Ingredients**

200g dark chocolate (something like Bourneville is fine, although you can of course go more fancy!)
150ml double cream
Flavouring(s) of your choice (will come back to this)
Melt the chocolate in a bowl using your preferred method, heat the cream until it bubbles up and add the cream to the bowl of melted

chocolate. Mix like crazy until it comes together as a glossy mass. This is known as a "ganache" - the gooey bit in the middle of the finished chocolate!

If you don't want a particular flavour, then just refrigerate the ganache as it is. Otherwise, decide how many flavours you want, divide up the mixture and add your flavourings, mix well and then refrigerate.

Once the ganache is firm, shape into balls using a melon baller, a spoon or your bare (clean) hands, or a combination of these implements.

At this point, you could just roll the balls in cocoa powder or grated chocolate and then refrigerate and they're ready to go. Or, you can refrigerate the balls again and when firm, coat them with the melted chocolate of your choice (e.g. I think milk chocolate goes nicely with the peanut butter ones, and white chocolate with raspberry…)

If you coat them immediately after shaping, the ganache might melt into the coating, but if you are pressed for time, you can do this. Once coated with melted chocolate, I like to sprinkle something "relevant" on top (e.g. freeze dried raspberries for a raspberry truffle, chopped toasted peanuts for peanut butter truffles, etc) for a bit of decorative flourish, but this is optional.

**Flavourings – here are some flavours I have used**

Peanut butter (about a dessert spoonful into half of the ganache mix)

Raspberry - push a handful of fresh raspberries through a sieve to extract the juice then heat the juice until it concentrates and reduces to a more syrupy texture

Coconut - melt a lump of "cream of coconut" and mix with the ganache.

Espresso - make a really strong cup of espresso and just use a teaspoonful or so

Ginger - get some stem ginger and mash it up

"Dark and stormy" - a bit of rum, lime zest and juice and stem ginger

Christmas spice – pinches of cinnamon, cloves, fresh nutmeg, ground ginger and some finely chopped orange zest.
Be careful with liquid flavourings, as they can loosen the ganache and make it hard to handle. You can reduce the amount of cream in the mix if using a liquid flavour, or reduce the liquid down so that it is more syrupy and less runny!

**Storage**

I tend to store these chocolates in the fridge, due to the cream content, but remove them from the fridge an hour or so before eating, as they are nicer at room temperature.

Suzie Withers

## Classic Vanilla Cupcake

Makes 12-15

## Ingredients

Cupcake: - 170g caster sugar
170g unsalted butter, softened
3 eggs, whisked
170g self-raising flour, sieved
1 tsp baking powder
1 ½ tsp vanilla extract
Topping: - 115g unsalted butter, softened
130g icing sugar, sieved
1tsp vanilla extract
Up to 1tbs milk
Preheat oven to 180 C

## Method

### Cupcake

In a large bowl cream together the caster sugar and butter until light and fluffy
Add eggs, vanilla extract and whisk until mixed
Fold flour and baking powder into mixture until creamy
Spoon the mixture into muffin cases until approx. 2 thirds full
Bake in the pre heated oven for 20-22 minutes until golden and spring back when lightly touched
Remove from baking tray and cool

### Buttercream Topping

Whisk the butter until pale in colour
Gradually add the icing sugar until all blended, light and creamy
Add vanilla extract and a little milk to the mixture and whisk. Adding a little more milk if needed
Pipe the buttercream topping onto the cakes and decorate.

Emma and Sue Brooks

# Spend Your Time Generously
# On Our Charitable Choices

Thanks to the Queen

Today as I dog walked what did I espy
A picture of the Queen's face staring square into my eye
As I walked closer to see what had occurred
Surprisingly something deep inside me stirred
'Never had you down as a Royalist' many people may say
No I'm not, my loyalties are with my friends most of the day
But this morning I am happy to appreciate our Queen
In my humble opinion in this picture she's the nicest she's ever been
It's brown and made of polymer, safe and strong and sound
A tenner I came across lying on the ground
I looked in front, I looked behind, but not a person was in sight
I bent quickly, my fingers they were light
I popped it in my pocket while I decided what to do
Could I honestly say it's mine, I didn't have a clue
Should I hand it in? Nobody will report it in this country lane
Shall I spend it 'cos I saved it from going down that filthy drain
Or shall I give it to a charity or to our New York account
To inflate our funds and make that a bigger more amazing amount

164

So thanks to our dear old Queen for helping with a round of beers
We all salute you Liz. Thanks from us Charioteers.

Jilly Firmin

## Charities That Sweet Charity Choir Have Supported

## Music Support

www.musicsupport.org
You are not alone. As a registered charity founded in April 2016, we provide vital help and support for individuals in all areas of the UK music industry suffering from alcoholism, addiction, emotional or mental health issues.

## By The Industry, For The Industry

We are dedicated to ensuring that all individuals working within music has access to support when suffering from addiction, emotional or mental health concerns.

## National Autistic Society

www.autism.org.uk
We are the UK's largest provider of specialist autism services. Our trained staff and volunteers bring passion and expertise to the lives of 100,000 autistic people every year.

## The Society Of St James

www.ssj.org.uk
Helping vulnerable people experiencing homelessness, problems with alcohol and substance use and other complex needs to change their lives. Hampshire's leading homelessness charity.

**Hope For Food**

www.hopeforfood.org.uk

**Helping The Needy In Bournemouth.**

Hope for Food is a local charity based in Bournemouth set up and run entirely by Volunteers. The organisation was founded by Claire Matthews in 2012 with the aim of providing life's basic essentials on a day to day basis to people in need of help due to the current economic climate.

**Alzheimer's Society**

www.alzheimers.org.uk
Alzheimer's Society is the only UK charity that campaigns for change, funds research to find a cure and supports people living with dementia today.

**Camvet Campaign**

https://camvet.vet.cam.ac.uk/Achievements/Camvetcampaign
Camvet is a small charity dedicated to raising funds for the Queen's Veterinary School Hospital in Cambridge. The hospital runs on a not-for-profit basis, so our goal is to fund essential equipment and facilities for diagnosing and treating the many thousands of animals referred for care. In addition, we help to fund teaching projects for our veterinary students. Every donation, no matter how large or small, really does make a huge difference to our animal patients.

**The Felix Project**

www.thefelixproject.org
The Felix Project collects fresh, nutritious food that cannot be sold. We deliver this surplus food to charities so they can provide healthy meals and help the most vulnerable in our society.

**Harp Homeless Charity**

www.harpsouthend.org.uk
HARP is the leading Southend charity helping local people overcome homelessness for good.

**Samaritans**

www.samaritans.org
We know a lot about what can help you through tough times. We can help you explore your options, understand your problems better, or just be there to listen.

**Dementia UK**

www.dementiauk.org
Dementia UK provides specialist dementia support for families through our Admiral Nurse service. Admiral Nurses provide the specialist dementia support that families need. When things get challenging or difficult, our nurses work alongside the entire family, giving them one-to-one support, expert guidance and practical solutions.

**Spread A Smile**

https://spreadasmile.org/
We spread smiles to seriously ill children and teenagers in hospital by providing entertainment including fairies, magicians, face-painters, singers, therapy dogs, children's characters, celebrities and theatre visits.

## Veterans With Dogs

www.veteranswithdogs.org.uk
We're helping Veterans with Post-Traumatic Stress Disorder (PTSD), and other mental health conditions, cope better with their symptoms and enabling them to lead more independent lives.

## Blue Cross For Pets

www.bluecross.org.uk
Pets are at the heart of everything we do. Each year, thousands of cats, dogs, small pets and horses turn to our animal hospitals, clinics and rehoming services for treatment and to find them the happy homes they deserve. Meanwhile, our Education and Behaviour Teams prepare future pet owners to take responsibility and look after their pets for life.

## MS Society

www.mssociety.org.uk
Together we campaign at all levels, fund ground-breaking research and provide award winning support and information.

## Water Aid

www.wateraid.org/uk
Extreme poverty won't end until everyone, everywhere has clean water, decent toilets and good hygiene.

## League Against Cruel Sports

www.league.org.uk
As an animal welfare charity, the League does everything we can to ensure that animals do not suffer for the sake of sport. Our motto sums up how we do it: Investigate, Educate, Protect.

## Macmillan Cancer Support

www.macmillan.org.uk
Whatever cancer throws your way, we're right there with you. We provide physical, emotional and financial support to help you live life as fully as you can.

## Streetwise Opera

www.streetwiseopera.org
Streetwise Opera is an award-winning performing arts charity for people who are or have been homeless. We run creative programmes in five regions across England and stage critically-acclaimed operas.

## The Red Box Project

www.redboxproject.org
The Red Box Project is a community-based, not-for-profit initiative, which aims to support young people throughout their periods by providing red boxes filled with free period products to local schools.

## Great ormond street.

www.gosh.org/webelieve
Every day, 619 children and young people from across the UK arrive at GOSH. Every day, doctors and nurses battle the most complex illnesses, and the brightest minds come together to achieve pioneering medical breakthroughs. And every day is a chance for you to make a difference.
This extraordinary hospital has always depended on charitable support to give seriously ill children the best chance to fulfil their potential. A better future for seriously ill children starts here.

**The Gift Of Life**

www.giftoflife.org
At Gift of Life we believe every person battling blood cancer deserves a second chance at life — and we are determined to make it happen. We are singularly passionate about engaging the public to help us get everyone involved in curing blood cancer, whether as a donor, a volunteer or a financial supporter. It all begins with one remarkable person, one life-changing swab and one huge win — finding a match and a cure.

**Parkinson's UK**

www.parkinsons.org.uk
We're the Parkinson's charity that drives better care, treatments and quality of life. Because we're here, no one has to face Parkinson's alone.

**Guide Dogs**

https://www.guidedogs.org.uk/
Our ambition is for a future where every person with sight loss has the confidence and support to live their lives to the full.

**CALM**

https://www.thecalmzone.net/
The Campaign Against Living Miserably (CALM) is leading a movement against male suicide, the single biggest killer of men under 45 in the UK. Join the campaign to take a stand against male suicide and get the tools you need for action.

## Lady Mcadden Breast Screening Trust

www.ladymcaddenbreastunit.co.uk
The charity aims to offer high quality services for the early detection of breast cancer through
mammography, examination and education in breast awareness and also by providing advice,
support, empathy and information, giving people the time and opportunity to discuss whatever concerns them.

## Margaret Green Animal Rescue

www.margaretgreenanimalrescue.org.uk
At Margaret Green Animal Rescue we take in pets that have become homeless due to a change in circumstances, or that have been neglected, mistreated or abandoned. Regardless of their circumstance, each pet will find a warm bed, a kind team and all the love and respect they deserve.

## The Royal British Legion

www.britishlegion.org.uk
The Royal British Legion provides lifelong support for the Armed Forces community - serving men and women, veterans, and their families.

## Bournemouth Hospital Charity

www.bhcharity.org
Bournemouth Hospital Charity exists to help enhance the care and treatment of our patients at the Royal Bournemouth and Christchurch Hospitals. The funds we raise through donations, gifts, legacies and our events help us to provide the Hospitals with additional facilities and state-of-the- art new equipment as well as resources for our staff, over and above what the NHS can fund.

171

**Kids Inspire**

https://kidsinspire.org.uk/
Kids Inspire helps disadvantaged young people turn their lives around and gives them back their future.

**Second Chance Animal Rescue**

www.secondchanceanimalrescue.co.uk
We are a small rescue that deals with dogs, cats, small animals, and wildlife. We have a dedicated team of volunteers that enable us to help as many animals as we possibly can. For over 30 years we have been helping animals find new homes that they can be happy in, but as always, there are more animals that need help than there are homes. Some of the many things we do here are: - to hand- raise orphaned animals, and in the case of wildlife, release them back into the wild when they are old enough; vaccinate and microchip all animals for rehoming, and treat any illness or injury of the animals in our care.

**The New Forest Trust**

https://www.newforesttrust.org.uk/
Formed in 2003 to secure the well-being of The New Forest for those who live in it and those who love it now and in the future.

**Back Up**

http://www.backuptrust.org.uk
Every 8 hours, someone in the UK is permanently paralysed. At Back Up, we inspire people affected by spinal cord injury to get the most out of life.

**Julia's House**

https://www.juliashouse.org/
We provide practical and emotional support for families caring for a child with a life-limiting or life-threatening condition, providing frequent and regular support in their own homes, in the community or at our hospices.

**End Youth Homelessness**

https://www.eyh.org.uk/en/
We have 4 main targets: housing, health, work and prevention. We want to raise national awareness and voluntary funds, ensuring a positive future for homeless young people.

**Donor Family Network**

https://www.donorfamilynetwork.co.uk/about-us/
It is our mission to become the leading donor family charity in the transplant community by providing awareness of organ donation and through the highest quality support for every donor family.It is our vision to promote the positive benefits of organ and tissue donation for the families of those who have died and donated, for recipients and for those awaiting transplants.

**James Mcmullan Support**

https://www.justgiving.com/crowdfunding/jamesmcmullan
James McMullan died in London terror attack. His sister says,
'It is important for us all to carry on with our lives in direct opposition to those who would try to destroy us.'

**Just Helping Children**

https://just4children.org/
Just4Children is passionate about the relief of sickness and preservation of health of children in the UK and Ireland by providing and assisting in the provision of grants to enable them to obtain medical treatment, therapies, living environments, equipment and holidays which would not otherwise be available to them.

**Dorset Rape Crisis Helpline**

https://www.dorsetrapecrisis.org/
To empower and enable anyone of any age, who has suffered from any sort of sexual violence or rape, or is supporting a survivor, to work with the trauma they have experienced and gain health to live their lives as they would wish.

**London Moonwalk**

https://walkthewalk.org/about-us
Uniting against breast cancer. Walk the Walk is the largest grant making breast cancer charity in the UK.

**Down's South**

http://downssouthlondon.org
Giving children with Down's Syndrome a head start.
A South London parent-run charity offering a unique, specialist early intervention therapy service for babies and young children with Down's Syndrome and a local support network for their families.

**Walk The Night**

https://www.dream-challenges.com/challenges/walk-the-night/
This epic night walk is the only event to bring men and women

together in exclusive support of the lifesaving prostate and breast cancer charities, Prostate Cancer UK and CoppaFeel!

**The £20 Challenge**

When we found out that a trip to Carnegie Hall in New York was on the cards for Sweet Charity Choir we were all so excited. What an amazing, once in a lifetime opportunity, and yet another chance to raise more money for charity.

It seemed it was all down to that beautiful Foo Fighters song 'Come Alive' and Jenny's moving arrangement.

We quickly realised it was going to take a bit of work to get all 150 of us there though. Of course we were all so happy to be going that we didn't mind paying our own way, but still, it was going to cost a pretty penny/dollar!

"Mmmmm," we thought, "It would be amazing if there was some money somewhere that we could put towards the airport transfers, or maybe a coffee for all of us."

"So what's the solution?" we asked ourselves.

One of our members, a bright spark called Shirley, came up with the idea of the £20 Challenge.

"Use your imagination," she said, "and come up with a way of making £20!"

So we did! We like a challenge, and this is what we came up with.....

- A talented artist offered to do a portrait as a raffle prize.
- A slimming challenge, 3 ladies have pledged to lose weight.
- Handmade knitted and crocheted items were sold.
- An invitation to friends and family to enjoy a homemade soup lunch. Super!
- An early Christmas dinner for friends.
- A raffle in one of our member's shop.
- A BINGO night.

- Donations for cakes and coffee at one of our member's bird watching group.
- Practice CD's were very popular to every member.
- Greeting cards and tags were made by a few members, and they were beautiful.
- Items were sold and money donated.
- A Thunder ball draw at work.
- A Fashion Show.
- Homemade chilli chutney. Yum!
- Karaoke and Cocktails. Hic!
- Afternoon tea and mini quizzes.
- One lovely member did the ironing and gardening for her neighbour. I wish she lived next door to me!
- Reflexology. So relaxing!
- A cryptic 'Sweeties' quiz and 'Jobs and Professions' quiz.
- A Murder Mystery evening.
- One member saved the money she would have spent on coffees when she's out.
- Babysitting.
- Sweets in handmade gift boxes were so cute.
- Homemade natural lip balm sale.
- Christmas dinner for 24 with a raffle - the winner got out of doing the washing up!
- Ladies night and coffee mornings.
- Various movie and dinner nights.
- A Curry night.
- A walk followed by afternoon tea.
- £1 a square with a monetary prize for the winner.
- Lyric songbooks. So useful.
- Sprinkles ice cream sundae evenings and a singsong.
- A bolognese evening and singsong.
- Bonus ball.
- Table Top sales.
- Car boot sales.
- Sweets in a jar challenge.

- Sweet Charity mugs and badges.
- Leftover coach money from our London busking day out, from Dorset/Hants and Southend choirs.
- And last but by no means least, a Fartathon by George!

All of these challenges were thought up individually by Sweet Charity members. They have given their time generously, and although it's a wonderful gesture of our fund raising choir, you can see it's not completely selfless. I'm sure we have all enjoyed our challenges along with our choir family, although maybe not George's particular challenge.... !

# Sit Back And Relax With Our
# Rhythmic Rhymes

A Day with Dermot

A trip to Southend in Essexshire, we're going to sing in a new choir

First of all I valet the car, more comfortable for passengers driving afar

First its Avril whose driven to the shop, but realised she's wrong so had to stop

Her sat nav isn't as good as mine, but now we've got Dermot we'll be just fine

Next stop is Tricia who we pick up on route, she puts all her bags and coat in the boot

Then to the pub to get Carol and Shirley, deep in the New Forest not far from Burley

Shirley is accompanied by a bottle of fizz, so if we get thirsty that will do the biz

My sat nav is narrated by a nice Irish man, who Shirley calls Dermot, her face dead pan

That sets the tone for the rest of the day, and we laughed about Dermot all the way

The idea's to stop for drinks and a wee, and a piece of cake to go with our tea

But some where on the journey we have to fit in food, we must try the local delicacy, not to would be rude

Dermot says 3 hours it will take, more with my driving for

goodness sake

But it feels like an hour with all the chat, and we've got Dermot to thank for that

Keep right, keep right, he constantly bellows, as I try to chat with my musical fellows

He doesn't shut up all the way, but that's an Irishman for you, hey

We need to practice our song for tonight, we need to make sure we get it right

A sop, a bass and 3 alto as we perform our tuneful concerto

5 part harmony singing right there, loud and proud without a care

The Dartford tunnel we speed under the water, which should help to make our journey shorter

Pleased with our progress, we're doing it large, but we didn't know how to pay the Dart Charge

Otherwise we drove right there who needs a man, if you can't do it Dermot can

We found a pizzeria for our dinner, Don Amici was really a winner

An Italian man who made us some tea, and his charm and attention was all given for free

Katherine was there and Claire and Suzie, and Colin of course, he's a right floozy

Ticking the register and enjoying the attention, surrounded by ladies, I feel I must mention

Jenny greeting and smiling so wide, you'd never guess she was nervous inside

She was singing so much she filled up with air, and politely let out a burp to share

I think they all loved her, the smiles on their cheeks, I'm sure they'll be back every week

They loved the refreshments the tea and cakes, I had 2 of the muffins that Cheryl makes

George was singing in the basses, with some of the lovely smiley faces

I've never heard him sing so low, I've nick-named him
George a Go Go
Time to leave Triple G and Jen, time is rolling and its getting
nearer to 10
11.30 pm and I'm needing a hit, so we stop for cappuccino
and a tit
Its actually a cherry Bakewell tart, and caffeine to keep me
awake is smart
Most people go to Southend on Sea with the notion, of fish
and chips eaten by the ocean
Not us, we visit to sing in a choir, and set Southend on Sea
on fire
Loved singing with this new Sweet Charity, Jenny will teach
them with humorous clarity
She'll take them all under her wing, and we'll all get
together for a Summer Big Sing

Jilly Firmin

**Nine years of notes, from A Bass, in A Choir.**

I've always loved music; I've always loved singing,
I could never describe the joy it keeps bringing.
I sing in the shower, I sing in the car,
But joining a choir, it's the best bit by far.
Way, way back, 2010 if I remember,
I found a choir that rocked, that September.
I had no idea of my vocal range,
So I thought I'd sing bass, just for a change!
"Hello, I'm Jenny, please take a seat."
She gave me a printed lyric sheet.
Her teaching, her humour, it went down a storm,
Before we knew it, we were fit to perform.
We froze in December, but escaped the snow,
We boiled in Brockenhurst at the New Forest Show.
The Regent Centre, Christchurch, the Approach at

Bournemouth Pier,
The Arena at Wembley beckoned the following year.
I will never forget that soggy day in July,
Singing in Southampton as the Olympic torch passed by.
Pretty soon we got chatting, so many friendly faces,
Caroline, Jan, Sue and Shelley, all my fellow basses.
We've cried, we've laughed, doubled over in stitches,
Whoever decided to name us Bass Bitches?
The years passed us by; we were all truly smitten,
Then Jenny, she left us, to go and sing with her Kittens.
What to do now? We gave it a year,
A new challenge we needed, that soon became clear.
"Singing with Jenny," the email had said,
It didn't take long for good news to spread!
Workshops to start with, just now and again,
Her arrangements so brilliant, they stuck in the brain.
Sweet Charity Choir was born; a monthly event,
We'd sing, eat cake and raise money, that's what it meant.
We recorded Come Alive, with a three-piece band and all,
Who knew it would soon lead us to Carnegie Hall!
So, roll on July it's off to New York we go,
And prepare to dazzle them with our Greatest Show!
I'm so pleased nine years on and we are all still singing,
I hope I've described how much joy it keeps bringing.
I'm still singing in the shower, I'm still singing in the car,
But singing with friends in a choir, it's the best bit by far!
We no longer wear black; we are ladies in navy blue,
Hopefully you can see how good singing is for you.
To be a poet like Jilly, I could never aspire,
These are just some old ramblings, from a bass, in a choir!!

Sarah Whiteside.

## The Ballad of Jenny D and SCC

A sassy young lady named Jenny
Whose talents were awesome, and many
Started a choir
Which aimed to inspire
And for charity raise the odd penny.
Sweet Charity Choir is its name
Friendship and fun was the aim
Then we sang "Come Alive"
With the message "Survive!"
And the choir quickly grew to acclaim
And now people started to see
We don't just eat cake and drink tea
A nice man called Roy
Said "Gee Whizz – Oh Boy –
Y'all coming to NYC"!
So Jenny, she answered the call
And now we're having a ball.
We've learned all our songs
And righted the wrongs
Now we're all off to Carnegie Hall!

Georgie Foord

## Once A Month

It all began in January of 2017.

I've been there from the beginning, to help realise Jenny's dream.
To get together every month and for charities some money make,
By singing, having fun and drinking tea - Oh, and eating lots of cake.

Rehearsals start with warm ups and a welcome to members new.

We may wiggle our arms, clench our bums and sing a tune or two.

Oohs and Aahs, Eews and Eehs our mouths go round and round.

Jen says we need to do this to make a better sound.

There's much anticipation when we begin a brand new song.

We are taught in harmony sections, but often get it wrong.

There is no need to worry, Jen's there to help us through,

By painting a picture in our minds or a unique visual clue.

A shoulder, an eyebrow, a hand or nod of the head

And into all our voices it slowly does embed.

We have lots of fun too, it's not all hard work.

We laugh, tell a joke and Jenny often burps.

Then it's all put together and our harmonies mingle.

An amazing arrangement that makes our spines tingle.

Soon it is time for a much needed break,

As for Jenny we work so hard.

There is always a rush to be front of the queue for a slice of Nick's roulade.

We make our donation then grab a drink,

But the goodies on the table often make us think.

Do we stuff ourselves with biscuits and cake,

Or grapes and melon if we're watching our weight?

Sometimes we get a visit from a charity or two.

The BBC were here one day - Briony and crew.

But usually it's just Jen and George-

He's her beau and the drummer of our band.

Jen tells us that he farts a lot but we never hear a sound.

George brings along his camera to take snaps and perhaps record.

He has a flashy tripod thing that he plays with when he's bored.

After the break we sit down and Jen has a chat.

She gives us the info about this and that.

Then it's back to the singing to finish the song.
A quick look at the clock tells us we don't have long.
By now though, we are all getting to know our parts
And the final run through we sing with our hearts.
3 hours has flown by, our session comes to an end.
It's time to stack up the chairs and say goodbye to our
friends.
But we know when we leave, and even in bed,
There'll be some bloomin' earworm going round in our
head.
Wherever this choir leads us, to ventures great or small.
A fundraiser in the Verwood Hub, or performing at Carnegie
Hall.
Supporting lots of charities, Big Sings and video shoots,
busking by the River Thames - we must always think back to
our roots.
To be part of a choir and the joy that it brings,
And once a month on a Sunday is where it begins.

Shirley Kavanagh

**New York Here I Come!**

I'm getting quite excited about our New York trip
I'm feeling fit to burst- come on Christine - get a grip!
I've still got so much to learn, so many of the songs
And when you really work it out, I haven't got that long!
So I'm giving up Smooth Essex for Sweet Charity instead
And with each little journey they're fixing in my head!
I have a problem with one or two- they're just so bloody sad
But as long as my tissues are handy it isn't quite so bad.
And other songs are wordy and my memory's not that hot
So repetition, repetition until the words I've got!
I'm trying hard to diet so I fit into my dress
But I cheat on every Tuesday, the cake's too good I must
confess!

So I'll go to New York fat, but as happy as can be
Cos I'm singing with my favourite choir- the amazing Sweet
Charity!

Christine Petherick

## Just Me

My life's been hard but I felt blest
So why did I get cancer of the breast?
I do not smoke, I do not drink
I exercise and make time to think.
Did I let it get me down and spiral into the depression
ground?
No, the cancer controlled me not
I stayed strong and I stayed proud
I went to work and faced the crowd.
But I was tired and I felt bruised, my silent thought I did
muse.
Now four years on it's time to tell of quiet internal living
hell
Fear was rife as lonely treatments I have borne
Every ache and pain triggered fear and scorn
Waves of anxiety occurred outright as I fought my way to
see the light
But should that cancer chance my way again
And I battle through the poison desolation game
My family need to know that whilst my love is over-
flowing
I need time to cry and let my anguish show
Come sit with me through countless tasks and cures
Lend me your determined strength as on this fearful journey
I vent
Give me your hope and a future to behold
Until the day I shout out loud that I've won the cancer battle
again

Until the day you hear me sing that I am here and I am JUST
ME.

Sara White

## When Tuesday Comes Around

Tuesday is my busiest day of the week by far
If they could bottle energy, I'd certainly buy a jar
And drink it down in one, not sip it like they say
I'd drink it with my breakfast to get me through the day
But as tired as the day makes me, when evening comes
around
I summon up the energy to go and make some sounds….
The Warm Up soon commences and 'oh and ah' begin
My mouth an open circle as I'm instructed to breath in.
Holding in my diaphragm, I let a small breath out
Hum a simple ditty to clear the cobwebs no doubt?
Up and down the scales we go, keeping eyes on Jenny.
I hope it's over quickly as I need to spend a penny.
Another sip of water and with my words to hand,
Eyes are fixed upon us, as my section has to stand!
Let us start with the chorus, oh joy... I haven't got a clue,
No time was had to practice, this one's completely new….
Will I understand my dots and dashes, squiggles and wavy
lines …
A sideways glance at my friend's sheet, hers is exactly the
same as mine.
We look at each other and shrug, trying not to laugh as we
both pretend we've done our homework but simply mouth
rhubarb!
We stop for cake and coffee, oh no let's carry on…
I will surely forget all that I've learned if this break goes on
too long.
A sing through once again brings it back without a fuss,
A riot of beautiful harmonies, is that really us!

Has it been ninety minutes, time really has flown past.
My tiredness has subsided, I have enjoyed this class.
Happy with my evening's work, I am homeward bound
But I simply cannot wait until next Tuesday comes around.

Lynn Gunter

## Sweet Charity Choir

Songs we love and cherish,
Whilst others keep us on our toes,
Excitement as we gather in the Hall.
Energy surrounds us, company and friendship,
Together as we listen, learn, recall.
Choir transcends our aches and pains,
Harmonies blend, troubles mend.
Age is just a word, voices to be heard,
Releasing our emotions:
Intense, funny, powerful and sad.
Tenacious teaching, talent and joy,
You know she's a star, we're so lucky, so glad.
Charity, Carnegie, chatting and cake,
How precious is this time and special bond.
Our Band enhances concerts, Olli's sound is so clever.
Inspirational Jenny, amazing and unique, may
Rehearsals of "SWEET CHARITY" last forever.

Sue Sissen

## Empire State of Mind Part 2

Empire State of Mind Part 2
Packed lunches, lyrics and clothes of blue
In our harmonies singing loud
While the band play to the noisy crowd
Jenny as usual on form

Amazing arrangement but that's the norm
'Ooh New York' sounds so sweet
Took a while to get it neat
But once we got it in our head
'It's time to record' Jenny said
That's if the band stops being bad
Lots of making up hugs were had
But we sing our song, the best take perhaps
Only for Papa Deacs to give some claps
Jenny collapsed laughing like a diva
Whilst Marianne waved her furry beaver
That's the perfect opportunity to stop for cake and a drink
The ladies did a sterling job I think
Back on the coach and all sungover
Although Becky and Kym may be hungover
On our way but why are the hazards flashing
And why's there a police car, although they're both quite
dashing
They're gonna give Nikki and I a lift to the pub
Maybe a drink and a bit of grub
Who knew we'd cause such a scene
And thanks to the rain, it's all looking green
Umbrellas on the hard shoulder ready for more rain
Next time we'll let the train take the strain

Jilly Firmin

# Jenny's Story

# Part Two

I believe in serendipity and am so certain the Rock Choir opportunity was a serendipitous moment for me. I was with Rock Choir for six years and honed and developed my skills as a musical director during that time. I loved being a part of Rock Choir and the reason I left was not because I didn't enjoy the job or didn't love the people I was teaching, far from it. I had this amazing opportunity to try a different avenue in the music industry with The Lounge Kittens. I knew I would regret it if I didn't at least try, but when it came to tell everyone, it was like breaking up with five hundred people, it was absolutely horrible. The agony of having to conceal it for three weeks, then tell everyone in my choirs and then finish the term, knowing that by the end of the term that would be it, was quite destructive.

I do not, treat my choir members as clients. They're my extended family, which for me is what makes it special. I'm not sure everyone should conduct their businesses in this way, as it is a huge responsibility - it can be a burden because you carry the weight of others' problems in their lives. It can be a really hard job to keep up and takes a very particular type of person to do this kind of a job, it's certainly not for everyone. It's in my nature to be completely inclusive - I wouldn't share anything with people that I wouldn't want them to know. I wouldn't invite people into my life unless I wanted them to be in it. I think when you give part of yourself to a group of people, they respect you more for it and want to do a better job. There are many Musical Directors out there who are very strict and critical and, whilst that can get fantastic results, I believe it is borne out of fear, which is not the way I do things. I don't want to be seen in that way and honestly, I don't think it's necessary - you can achieve the same results being relatable.

The year after I left RC, I was submerged into a totally different side of the music industry and it felt like I was allergic to it. In the commercial side of the music industry, you have to portray yourself like a product that everyone NEEDS and act as though you're the most important person in the room, that everyone should be begging you for your time and I just hated it.

We had a really hard time during that year in as much as we did everything by the book and were let down by people who were supposed to be working with us. We had so much of the responsibility on our shoulders which ultimately took away some of the enjoyment out of what we were doing. It's more hard work than people realise, emotionally and physically, you have to have thick skin, take on all the criticisms and then be really humble whilst still being prominent about all your achievements. It is a whirlwind of emotions and status against a backdrop of hard slog. I felt very detached from the real world because we were in our own little bubble and it was all-encompassing.

I don't think I had fully considered the impact of leaving my choir members. I still miss the team ethic and camaraderie from Rock Choir of course, but more than that I was missing the people that I interacted with on a weekly basis and I missed teaching them. I began to realise that a piece of my soul and a bigger piece of my self-worth was missing from not doing that job anymore. The bit that made me feel I should be on this planet wasn't there anymore. That, coupled with the hardship of The Lounge Kittens over those twelve months, meant that I just felt totally worthless by the end of the year and I was absolutely skint. I was living in London with Mum and Dad (THANK YOU!) and I had nothing, but it was when I met George.

We have a mutual friend Andrew Small, who is a Rock Choir leader (and now guitarist for Sweet Charity Choir!). George was the drummer in Andrew's previous function band *Happy Hour,* and they played at my Rock Choir leaving do, which is when I first officially met George. I think we managed to say "Hi" that night. Oooh, the romance! Later in 2016, when TLK were recording our album, we hired *Happy Hour* to perform on our Prodigy Medley. That's when we met properly and spent time with each other in the studio. Again serendipitous, because George didn't learn his music properly, so I had to teach him 'on the fly' and instructed that he didn't take his eyes off me for the duration of recording. Truth be told, I was not happy with him! But it did mean we kept eye contact throughout the whole day in the studio... After that, we started talking on Facebook, then exchanged numbers. We were clearly flirting with each other and about a month later we went on a date. And the rest is history!

I would talk about choir with him in those early days and he encouraged me to re-evaluate my life and seriously consider what I would do once the contractual year of not teaching choirs came to an end. My feeling was that I needed to re-attach myself to the world and to do what made my heart sing. I came up with the idea of Sweet Charity Choir (without it actually being called Sweet Charity at this point) as a one-year project called *Sing to Save*. This was to be an opportunity to make a little bit of money doing something that I loved and I knew I was good at, but more importantly to be able to see everyone and sing with everyone again. I realised then that this is what made me happy.

I think at that first session in Dorset, we had about forty people come along. I publicised it on my public profile pages on Facebook, so anyone who saw it could make their own decision to sign up if they were interested. Immediately, during that first session, I felt that part of me was rebuilding and over time I could feel my karma cup (which I had s* * ** * *t all over during that first year after leaving Rock Choir) beginning to fill up. Over the year, the choir grew gradually and organically and by the end of the year we had about eighty singers. Every month we would choose a different charity to support through tea and cake and that way I felt like we were giving back to the world.

I had finally found my happy place: I got to see people I had missed terribly after a year of absence, I managed to earn a bit of money and found a way give back to the universe, which ultimately made me feel whole.

Although we had been meeting up once a month, in our first year we didn't have enough material or rehearsal time to put on a concert so I decided to round off the year with a big recording day where we could record everything we had learned so far accompanied by a live band, which no one had experienced before. I decided to tie in my idea for 'Come Alive' on the same day.

The 'Come Alive' video came about around the same time that we lost two greats in the music industry to suicide, Chris Cornell and Chester Bennington. I didn't know them personally, but their music was such a huge part of my teenage years and I found it so distressing to think that two people with such success and who afforded so much admiration across the world could take their own lives. Depression is a silent killer, and many don't realise it. Thankfully the conversations are starting now through campaigns and advertisements, corporations and charities, but there is still a long way to go.

I originally wrote the arrangement of 'Come Alive' because the lyrics spoke to me personally about my depression, and with the loss of Chris and Chester, it clicked in my head. I wanted to do something, even if no one saw it but choir members and their loved ones. I thought that if I connected to the song about mental health, then potentially millions of other people could, and it encouraged me to do something to raise awareness for people in the music industry who are living under the spotlight under the stress of touring.

It was Julie Wootten in the Dorset Choir who brought Music Support UK to my attention. It is a charity for people who work in the music industry, run by people in the music industry. They give judgement-free help for people who are experiencing difficult tour life, mental health issues or substance abuse and they even provide legal advice. This is all provided by people who understand the trials and tribulations of working in the music industry - they understand and can be the voice or ear to someone in need.

I decided Music Support would be showcased in the video, but I didn't want to alienate any other charity who weren't based in the UK or in the music industry. After much consideration, I thought the most accessible suicide crisis charity worldwide would be the Samaritans. They were incredibly helpful to someone close to my heart and thought that on a global scale, this would be the best course of help for everybody. We made the video with the idea that if we reached even one person and it prompted them to pick up the phone to talk to someone, reach out to a friend behaving abnormally, or just educate people about a worldwide epidemic, then it would be worth doing.

Never did we envisage or have the intention of it going viral. I still to this day cannot believe it and once again, serendipity played a part! The video did go viral and it reached the attention of Dave Grohl, who endorsed it on the Foo Fighters' social media platforms, which was absolutely mind-blowing! It has also led us to Carnegie Hall - our first ever over-seas performance in New York City! Dr Roy Hayes, the director of True North Presents events company, is a huge Foo Fighters fan and came across our video on YouTube. It was our video that prompted him to contact me and start this awesome, bucket list, once in a lifetime adventure!.

I asked my members if they wanted the choir to continue and, luckily, I was welcomed with a resounding YES! The name Sweet Charity Choir came from Dorset member Georgie Foord, suggesting it because it encompasses our love of singing, baking and raising money for charity - and so Sweet Charity Choir was officially born! In January 2018, I launched the Southend SCC, full of spritely, ballsy, caring and hilarious singers and, in September 2018, the Hampshire SCC was launched with hard-working, sweet, kind-hearted, and wonderful singers.

I'm constantly overwhelmed with the amount of love we each have surrounding us in our choir communities - I URGE people to get out in your local towns and find a choir, it could be the best decision of your life!

*"If you are presented with an opportunity - say yes and work out how to do it later" - Richard Branson*

I have lived my whole adult life by this Richard Branson quote, even if it means I make mistakes but learn from them.

I am at the point now where I feel I have a real vision. I am already in the process of branching out, with potentially three future leaders who are going to set up their own Sweet Charity Choirs in their own towns. It feels incredible and certainly wasn't something I set out to do, it has just happened organically. My Bass Guitarist, Kurt, expressed to me he wanted to be a leader, and he is absolutely the right type of person for the job. We start training after Carnegie Hall! We made a deal that he plays Bass for my choirs and I'll play Bass for his choirs! Yes, I am going to learn bass! The plan is for Kurt to open his choirs in the North of Essex into Suffolk.

I have got a five-year plan… and without spilling the beans I intend to perform in other countries in Europe as well as some iconic venues in the UK, record at some pretty cool places and say YES when I'm presented with something fun for the choir. As always, I will find a way to make *something* happen!

Jenny Deacon

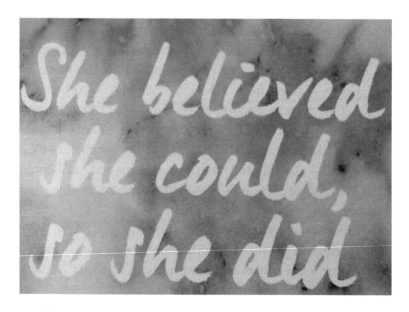

# Special Thanks

"My musical and personal growth would not be possible without every person mentioned and involved in this book, but a few special mentions are required!

My wonderful family - thank you for seeing something within me and encouraging me to follow what I felt was right. I have the best role models in one family unit and I wouldn't be the person I am today if it wasn't for you all.

George - thank you for always lifting me up, pushing me to my limits, loving not only me but the choirs whole heartedly. And to George's family for always being a positive light in my life.

Harrow Young Musicians - for showing me the possibilities of the musical world and allowing me to be a part of it from such a young age.

Olli - for understanding my musical brain in a way that we don't even have to use words to get a job done. Your passion and enthusiasm towards everything I do with the choir as well as myself personally encourages me to do more.

Lucy, Andy, Josh, Kurt, George - my SCC band of extraordinary musicians. We are all lucky to have you in our team.

Marianne Harris, Scott Chalmers and Corinne Cumming for their fabulous photos.

Kelly and Jilly - for their tireless work on this book. I can't imagine how many hours have been put into creating this beautiful nugget of choir life; you're both angels!

The Reddit and Youtube Community - for recognising the beauty of the choir and spreading the music!"

Jenny Deacon

If you have been affected by any of the stories contained within this book, or you would like further information and support regarding Mental Health and Well-being, please visit the following links:

*Mental Health UK:*
https://mentalhealth-uk.org/help-and-information/

*BBC:*
https://www.bbc.co.uk/programmes/articles/1NGvFrTqWChr03LrY lw2Hkk/information-and-support-mental-health

*Time to Change:*
https://www.time-to-change.org.uk/

*Samaritans:*
https://www.samaritans.org/about-samaritans/our-organisation/what-we-do/

# Members of Sweet Charity Choir

# MEMBERS OF SWEET CHARITY CHOIR

Anna Allen

Alexia Anderson

Katy Anderson

Julia Archer

Sarah Ashurst Williams

Clare Bailey

Penny Baker

Sharon Ball

Shelagh Barber

Diane Barker

Steve Barney

Rosie Barrett

Susan Bates

Charmaine Beale

Lynda Beale

Naomi Beer

Elaine Bell

Mick Bellini

Mandy Belton

Hannah Bennett

Susan Berry

Sue Boardman

Sarah Borowski

Sally Bowman

Kathryn Boydell

Maggie Bracher

Sandi Bradshaw

Barbara Brady

Emma Brooks

Sue Brooks

Tina Buckland

Daniela Cajales

Denise Carroll

Sue Carter

Jan Christofi

Rachel Cholerton

Maggie Clarke

Carol Coates

Pauline Cornish

Jean Cox

Lydia Crowe

Pauline Crowe

Iokasti Curry
Colin Daniels
Karen Dalmasi
Gill Davies
Lee Day
Marion Deacon
Jenny Devine
Sue Divall
Janet Dixon
Teresa Dobson
Debbie Drake
Val Durrant
Tricia Edwards
Jill Ewens
Maxine Farmer
Jilly Firmin
Sandra Fish
Alison Fityan
Carol Fitzgerald
Annie Fleming
Colin Fleming
Georgie Foord
Louise Ford
Jane Forrest
Linda Fountain
Julie Fowles
Jo Frampton
Jane Francis
Mary Franklin
Sarah Fryer
Sharon Funk
Louise Gabony
Jan Galton
Jane Gates
Lesley Gee
Kay Geoghegan

Pat Gossling
Sally Grant
Angie Gray Adams
Jan Gregory
Beryl Grindrod
Becky Guest
Lynn Gunter
Susan Hacker
Kim Haddrell
Kim Hamilton
Carol Harris
Deb Harris
Deborah Harris
Sue Harris
Claire Harrison
Linda Harrison
Lizzie Harrison
Katie Hawkins
Mark Hemington
Gerry Henley
Pauline Henry
Christine Hensser
Annabel Hentall MacCuish
Sheila Hentall
Laura Hewett
Sue Hibberd
Sue Hirst
Sarah Holleran
Sally Holman
Sue Holton
Julie Hope
Olive Hopkins
Gary Howard
Claire Hoyal
Tessa Huckstep
Pat Hudson

# MEMBERS OF SWEET CHARITY CHOIR

Diane Hunt
Melanie Hunt
Natasha Jarvis
Kathryn John-Mosse
Louise Johnson
Shelley Joyce
Pippa Judd
Shirley Kavanagh
Claire Keay
Gina Kent
Diane Kimber
Margaret Kimmens
Deborah Klayman
Alex Lai
Natalie Laishley
Helen Langdown
Sue Lawrence
Nicky Laverton
Jean Lay
Linda Lee
Celeste Le-Mare
Jan Lewis
Chris Linard
Angela Lloyd
Patricia Lloyd
Beck Lombardi
Tina Loughlin
Emma Lucas
Karen Lucas
Michelle Lucas
Pat Lytheer
Kerrie Malandreniotis
Debbie Mantle
Avril Martin
Maureen Martin
Kym Mason

Rick Mawdsley
Gail Maxted
Nick McCullen
Gill McGrath
Moira McGrath
Mary McKenzie
Chris Mears
Jo Melder
Kerrie Merrett
Tiffany Miramon
Pip Moore
Crystal Morgan
Rachel Morse
Sue Newbold
Tracey Newman
Gwen Newton
Dilys Nicholls
Chris Noonan
Anne Norton
Carol Offord
Juliette Otton
Rhiann Owen
Angela Pallett
Jenny Park
Erika Parkinson
Maggie Parma
Sandy Partridge
Claire Pearce
Ash Pearson
Karen Pearson
Dominic Perry
Christine Petherick
Owen Phillips
Richard Phillips
Sally Phillips
Julia Picking

Rachel Pitman
Sophie Plant
Stef Pope
Susie Porter
Carol Potter
Kat Powell
Sheena Prescott
Nicky Radziusz
Emma Read
Jan Renton
Kelly Reynolds
Sarah Richards
Pam Ripley
Maureen Robb
Katherine Robertson
Carole Robinson
Jenny Robinson
Coral Rogers
Sheila Rogers
Nuala Rosenvinge
Lise Rossano
Natalie Rowe
Kathy Rushton
Shirley Rutland
Sharon Savage
Charlie Say
Cheryl Say
Sarah Sennett
Jackie Sewell
Carolyn Sherwin
Sue Sissen
Jean Shuler-Turner
Tracey Sibthorpe
Geraldine Skinner
Jo Smith
Elena Sneddon

Janet Solecki
Nikki Soulsby
Janis Southern
Jennifer Spencer
Valerie Stenson
Lisa Stephens
Dawn Stevens
Rachel Strange
Denny Sullivan
Karen Tappenden
Jane Taylor
Rachel Taylor
Regina Teo
Maya Tipper
Gill Tobin
Alison Tonna
Sandy Trapnell
Jane Trew
Jackie Turner
Catrin Turrell
Rachel Tyler
Patricia Ullett
Caron Uzzell
Astrid Vaswani
Becks Vince
Nicola Walker
Jane Walters
Sheelagh Wanstall
Emma Wareham
Susan Warriner
Laura Werling
Eileen Westley
Kathy White
Sara White
Jenni Whiteman
Roy Whiteman

# MEMBERS OF SWEET CHARITY CHOIR

Sue Whiten

Sarah Whiteside

Alan Whitty

Karen Whitty

Marion Wicks

Nerissa Wilkins

Emma Williams

Mary Williams

Polly Williams

Tracey Williams

Sue Wilson

Suzie Withers

Caroline Wood

Claire Wood

Hannah Woodford

Carol Woolf

Julie Wootten

Ann Wright

Rachel Wyeth

Katie Yeates

Fay Young

Lisa Young

L - #0088 - 150819 - C0 - 234/156/12 - PB - DID2590891